MW00573013

CANADA
ALONE

Kim Nossal (signature)

CANADA ALONE

NAVIGATING THE POST-AMERICAN WORLD

KIM RICHARD NOSSAL

DUNDURN
PRESS

Copyright © Kim Richard Nossal, 2023

All rights reserved. No part of this publication may be reproduced, stored in a retrieval system, or transmitted in any form or by any means, electronic, mechanical, photocopying, recording, or otherwise (except for brief passages for purpose of review) without the prior permission of Dundurn Press. Permission to photocopy should be requested from Access Copyright.

Publisher: Kwame Scott Fraser | Acquiring editor: Kathryn Lane | Editor: Carrie Gleason
Cover designer: Karen Alexiou
Cover image: MrWildLife/shutterstock.com

Library and Archives Canada Cataloguing in Publication

Title: Canada alone : navigating the post-American world / Kim Richard Nossal.
Names: Nossal, Kim Richard, author.
Description: Includes bibliographical references and index.
Identifiers: Canadiana (print) 20230444644 | Canadiana (ebook) 20230444679 | ISBN 9781459752450 (softcover) | ISBN 9781459752474 (EPUB) | ISBN 9781459752467 (PDF)
Subjects: LCSH: Canada—Foreign relations—1945- | CSH: Canada—Foreign relations—21st century.
Classification: LCC FC242 .N678 2023 | DDC 327.71—dc23

We acknowledge the support of the Canada Council for the Arts and the Ontario Arts Council for our publishing program. We also acknowledge the financial support of the Government of Ontario, through the Ontario Book Publishing Tax Credit and Ontario Creates, and the Government of Canada.

Care has been taken to trace the ownership of copyright material used in this book. The author and the publisher welcome any information enabling them to rectify any references or credits in subsequent editions.

The publisher is not responsible for websites or their content unless they are owned by the publisher.

Printed and bound in Canada.

Dundurn Press
1382 Queen Street East
Toronto, Ontario, Canada M4L 1C9
dundurn.com, @dundurnpress 𝕏 f ⊙

For Colin, Rowan, and Liam

CONTENTS

CONTENTS

ABBREVIATIONS

ACEUM	Accord Canada–États Unis–Mexique
AFPAC	America First Political Action Conference
AKP	*Adalet ve Kalkınma Partisi* (Justice and Development Party)
ALP	Australian Labor Party
AFPI	America First Policy Institute
ANZUS	Australia, New Zealand, United States Security Treaty
APEC	Asia-Pacific Economic Cooperation
ASEAN	Association of Southeast Asian Nations
AUKUS	Australia–United Kingdom–United States security partnership
BRI	Belt and Road Initiative
CCF	Co-operative Commonwealth Federation
CPAC	Conservative Political Action Conference
CPC	Communist Party of China
CPTPP	Comprehensive and Progressive Agreement for Trans-Pacific Partnership
CSIS	Canadian Security Intelligence Service
CUSMA	Canada–United States–Mexico Agreement
DEPA	Digital Economy Partnership Agreement
EAS	East Asia Summit
EIU	Economist Intelligence Unit
EU	European Union
FCC	Federal Communications Commission

FVEY	Five Eyes intelligence alliance
G7	Group of Seven
G20	Group of Twenty
GOP	Grand Old Party (Republican Party)
IJC	International Joint Commission
INF	Intermediate-Range Nuclear Forces
INTERPOL	International Criminal Police Organization
IPEF	Indo-Pacific Economic Framework for Prosperity
MAGA	Make America Great Again
NAFTA	North American Free Trade Agreement
NATO	North Atlantic Treaty Organization
NDP	New Democratic Party
NORAD	North American Aerospace Defense Command
OIF	Organisation internationale de la Francophonie
P5	Permanent 5 members of the UN Security Council
PBP	Partners in the Blue Pacific
PLA	People's Liberation Army
POTUS	President of the United States
PRC	People's Republic of China
RINO	Republican in name only
SOE	State-owned enterprise
SOS	Secretary of State Coalition
SSN-AUKUS	AUKUS nuclear-powered submarine
T-MEC	Tratado entre México, Estados Unidos y Canadá
TPP	Trans-Pacific Partnership
USMCA	United States–Mexico–Canada Agreement
USSR	Union of Soviet Socialist Republics (Soviet Union)
WTO	World Trade Organization
WWG1WGA	Where we go one, we go all

PROLOGUE

For four days the 2020 American presidential election was simply too close to call. After the polls in the Aleutian Islands finally closed in the early hours of November 4, President Donald J. Trump immediately claimed that he had won re-election. But, as the ballots were counted over the next few days, his Democratic opponent, Joe Biden, kept slowly accumulating Electoral College votes. The end came suddenly — and precisely: at 11:25 a.m. Eastern Time on Saturday, November 7, 2020, the Associated Press called Pennsylvania for Joe Biden. With Biden leading in that state by more than 34,000 votes, and with just 62,000 mail ballots to be counted, AP judged that Trump could not win the state's popular vote. Pennsylvania's twenty Electoral College votes would instead go to Biden, propelling him past the magic number of 270 votes needed to take the presidency from Trump.

As the news that Joe Biden would be the next president spread around the world that Saturday afternoon, political leaders in other countries of the West — allies and friends of the United States — began to issue formal statements congratulating Biden and his running mate, Kamala Harris. However, these were messages with an edge. The wording that they used in their official statements, their tweets, or their media hits left little doubt that these leaders were deeply relieved that Trump had gone down to defeat. Only Benjamin Netanyahu, prime minister of Israel, had anything nice to say about the soon-to-be-former president. The rest were clearly anticipating that on January 20, 2021, the Trump presidency — along with its idiosyncratic diplomacy, its "America First" policies, its denigration of international institutions, and the president's personal attacks on other world leaders — were all going to be a thing of the past. Anne Hidalgo, the mayor of Paris, probably spoke for most Western leaders when she tweeted, "Welcome back America!"[1]

Nowhere was that relief more keenly felt than in Ottawa. The Liberal government of Justin Trudeau had spent four years trying hard to manage Trump's attacks on the international order, on Canadian economic interests, and, as concerning, on Canadian politicians. Trump had come to office with a deep skepticism about America's alliances. He was a confirmed protectionist. He strongly believed that countries like Canada were just pretending to be friends and allies while eagerly ripping off long-suffering Americans through unfair trading practices and refusing to spend enough on defence. Trump had come to the White House in January 2017 convinced that the North American Free Trade Agreement, signed by Canada, Mexico, and the United States in 1993, was a "disaster," a "catastrophe," and a "nightmare." He repeated his signature description of NAFTA as "the worst trade deal ever made" on numerous occasions, and promised during the 2016 election campaign that as president he would either renegotiate the agreement or just "break it."

Trump was as good as his word. His administration arbitrarily imposed tariffs on Canadian steel and aluminum, using a provision in American law that allows the president to levy duties on imports that are deemed to threaten American national security. The idea that Canada posed a national security threat to the United States was, of course, absurd, but it fit well with Trump's protectionist views. And his administration successfully renegotiated a new trade agreement with Canada and Mexico. When he signed it into law in January 2020, Trump proclaimed that he was "ending the NAFTA nightmare" — even though the new agreement looked very similar to the "nightmare" it was replacing. But Trump could point to the concessions that both Canada and Mexico had agreed to as the price for maintaining access to the United States market. And he could also point to the new name he had given it: the United States–Mexico–Canada Agreement (USMCA), which symbolically made no mention of free trade, but also, in a nod to Trump's "America First" agenda, listed the United States first. The other signatories responded to this name-gamesmanship by playing the same game with the bizarre result that the new agreement goes by different legal names in each of the three countries: it is USMCA for Americans, but T-MEC (Tratado entre México, Estados Unidos y Canadá) in Mexico, and CUSMA (Canada–United States–Mexico Agreement) and ACEUM (Accord Canada–États Unis–Mexique) in Canada.

As important was the deterioration in the personal relationship between Trump and Trudeau. While personal relations between American presidents and Canadian prime ministers have sometimes been marked by disagreements over policy, or by personality clashes, the public expression of Trump's anger at Trudeau marked a distinct historical departure. The low point came in June 2018, when the president, annoyed at a comment that Trudeau had made at a press conference about American tariffs, mean-tweeted that the prime minister was "very dishonest & weak." In December 2019, when Trudeau was caught on a hot mic laughing about Trump with other leaders at a North Atlantic Treaty Organization (NATO) summit in London, the president responded by calling Trudeau "two-faced." But Trudeau was not the only target of Trump's anger:

in September 2018, the president also criticized Chrystia Freeland, Canada's foreign minister, telling supporters at a fundraiser that she "hated America," and calling her "a nasty woman."[2]

Given how fraught the Canada–United States relationship became during the Trump presidency, it is hardly surprising that Trudeau's formal message of congratulations was framed in traditional hands-across-the-border rhetoric: "Canada and the United States enjoy an extraordinary relationship — one that is unique on the world stage. Our shared geography, common interests, deep personal connections, and strong economic ties make us close friends, partners, and allies." But Trudeau also evoked all those policy issues that had been spurned by Trump: "We will further build on this foundation as we continue to keep our people safe and healthy from the impacts of the global COVID-19 pandemic, and work to advance peace and inclusion, economic prosperity, and climate action around the world."[3]

After Biden was inaugurated on January 20, 2021, Trudeau was the first leader to have a substantive telephone conversation with the new president. They discussed a range of policy issues: collaboration on vaccines; action on climate change and net-zero emissions; expanded cooperation on continental defence and the modernization of the North American Aerospace Defense Command (NORAD). They discussed the cases of Michael Kovrig and Michael Spavor, two Canadians arrested in China in retaliation for the arrest of Meng Wanzhou, chief financial officer of Huawei Technologies, on an extradition request by the United States. They talked about trade, supply chain resilience, and barriers to trade. Trudeau expressed his concern about the American refusal to approve the Keystone XL pipeline.

A month later the two leaders had their first summit meeting, accompanied by Vice-President Kamala Harris and Chrystia Freeland, the deputy prime minister, together with Antony Blinken,

Biden's secretary of state, and Marc Garneau, Canada's foreign minister. Because of COVID-19, it was a virtual meeting. In their introductory prepared remarks delivered in front of the media, Biden and Trudeau stressed the importance of working together on global issues. Indeed, Trudeau went out of his way to praise the Biden administration's policy toward climate change. "Thank you again for stepping up in such a big way on tackling climate change," he said. "U.S. leadership has been sorely missed over the past — past years. And I have to say, as — as we're preparing the — the joint rollout and communiqué from this one, it's nice when the Americans are not pulling out all references to climate change and, instead, adding them in."[4] The meeting ended with the adoption of a twelve-page "Roadmap for a Renewed U.S.-Canada Partnership" that outlined how a range of cross-border issues would be dealt with.

This virtual summit meeting very much reflected the priority that the Biden administration attached to returning the Canadian-American relationship to a degree of civility and predictability that had been so absent during the Trump years, and presaged its broader efforts to undo the damage that Trump had done to relations with America's friends and allies. But the meeting was also notable for how different it was from the previous administration: here were political leaders who delivered carefully scripted statements; they focused on important policy issues; agreements had been reached by bureaucrats on both sides of the border who spent time prior to the summit working out agreed-upon language; they discussed points of disagreement between their two governments civilly and with a view to resolving differences; they stressed jointness, cooperation, and alignment.

Perhaps that is why a common reaction of officials in Ottawa was happiness at just how *normal* this summit was after four years of craziness. And profound relief that the United States was back.[5]

INTRODUCTION

The Liberal government of Justin Trudeau might well have breathed a collective sigh of relief when Joe Biden was inaugurated as the 46th U.S. president in 2021. It seemed like American foreign policy would be more or less back to normal. For under Biden America is indeed "back" in global politics. Biden's foreign-policy instincts are what students of the discipline of International Relations call internationalist — in other words, he believes that countries should best defend their interests in world politics by being actively engaged rather than seeking isolation and withdrawal. He believes in multilateralism — the idea that the United States should work with others, in particular its friends and allies, to solve global problems. He believes in America's alliances, and values those allies. He believes in the idea of American leadership in global politics. And his administration is run by senior officials who are expert foreign affairs professionals, and committed not only to a particular conception of world order, but also, like their boss, to the importance of exercising global leadership to maintain it.

The Trudeau government's foreign policy reflected this return to normality. The government in Ottawa sought to work with the Biden administration at a multilateral level on a range of issues, including climate change and pandemic response. Ottawa welcomed the leadership shown by the Biden administration in rallying the West's response to the Russian Federation's full-scale invasion of Ukraine that began in February 2022. In the fall of 2022, the Trudeau government shifted its policy to align Canada more closely to American policies toward the People's Republic of China (PRC). It began to spend more on defence, including modernizing the North American Aerospace Defense Command (NORAD) and finally committing to purchasing a fleet of eighty-eight F-35 jet fighters. It has downplayed the progressive foreign policy agenda that it tried to pursue in 2016 and 2017. Canadian foreign policy today is very much premised on the assumption that the Trump years are well and truly in the past.

However, to assume that Trump or Trumpism is behind us would be to ignore what is happening in the United States. The shifts in American politics that propelled Donald J. Trump to the White House in 2017 have not disappeared. On the contrary: the persistence of the trends in American politics and foreign policy that Trump had both reflected and inspired remain very much in evidence. In domestic politics the Republican Party — or "Grand Old Party" (GOP) — has experienced a profound anti-democratic and illiberal lurch under Trump and his Make America Great Again (MAGA) movement. The longer-term political effects of the armed insurrection on January 6, 2021, that Trump and his allies incited after he lost the 2020 election are yet to be fully felt. Nor do we know the effects of the sustained efforts by the GOP to deny the legitimacy of the 2020 election, or the spread of extremism in the Republican Party in 2021 and 2022.

Most importantly, we will not know whether, in the years ahead, the United States will continue to play a leadership role in world politics — the kind of role it played for all but four of the last eighty years. Many of Trump's ideas about world politics, captured most vividly in his slogan "America First," generated such enthusiasm during his presidency precisely because they were a variant of a long-standing approach to world affairs in the United States, called the conservative-nationalist tradition in American foreign policy.[1] The conservative-nationalist approach is marked by an intense focus on advancing the interests of the United States by maximizing the country's autonomy in global politics. That means rejecting any of the limits on American sovereignty and freedom of maneuver that multilateral involvement impose, and instead encouraging a persistent skepticism about international institutions. It also means seeking to "win" in international affairs: in other words, never yielding to adversaries, always rejecting concessions to others, and generally acting, in the words of the foreign minister of one middle power who found himself at the receiving end of American unilateralism, "without regard to the legitimate interests of others."[2] The conservative-nationalist nature of Trump's America First agenda was popular with Americans; its popularity will not diminish.

We can see evidence of this after Trump's defeat in 2020. While the Biden administration has worked hard to reverse much of the damage done to American foreign policy by the Trump administration, it has also left many of Trump's policies in place, particularly the protectionist measures imposed on both friends and adversaries alike. Likewise, the Democratic Party's approach to the rise of China as a great power, and its efforts to contain China, differ from Trumpist policies only in the level of professionalism and competence of the Biden team.

The possibility that we will see the resurgence of a conservative-nationalist trend in American foreign policy has profound implications for global politics — and for Canada, since our foreign and defence policies are designed for a world in which the United States plays a leadership role in shaping a particular kind of world order. But what if we see a resumption of the kind of profound transformations in American foreign policy that began in 2017, and were only interrupted by Trump's defeat in 2020? In that event, those shifts in foreign policy are likely to have more lasting impacts on global politics. If that happens, the kind of foreign policy being pursued by the Trudeau government will have been overtaken by events, since the world it was designed for will have been transformed.

The purpose of this book is to explore the implications for Canadians of such a transformation. We need to begin by looking backwards in order to understand why Canada is at such a fraught crossroads. In Chapter 1 we look at the world that Canadians have been used to living in since the end of the Second World War. That world — the American-led rules-based international order — was, unambiguously, an *American* world, reflecting the power and centrality of the United States in shaping global politics. Judging by their persistent political support for remaining part of that world, Canadians clearly saw the American-led international order — and the systemic peace and increasing wealth that came with it, at least for some in the world — working in their interests.

But we will also explore a key paradox in Canada's case: over the last eighty years, Canadians have never seen themselves as part of an "American world," but always as part of a larger grouping of states. For Canada has always understood that being a member of a larger group offers a small country in global politics substantial benefits. Being a member of a group provides strength in numbers. It also affords smaller countries the opportunity to search with other like-minded countries for multilateral solutions to global problems and gives small countries a "seat at the table" in global discussions with great powers. And in Canada's case, there was the additional advantage of being able to deal with the United States in this company.

Over the last decade, however, the American world has been under sustained assault. In Chapter 2, we begin with a look at the two broad developments in global politics over the last ten years that have posed major challenges to the American world: the growth of Russian revanchism and the rise of an aggressively assertive China. But Russian and Chinese efforts to displace American leadership only tells us part of the story. To understand how, and why, the American world has been so shaken, we need to look at a third development in contemporary global politics: the rise, paradoxically, of a U.S. president who lacked the commitment of all his predecessors (and his immediate successor) to American global leadership. On his first full day in office, Trump set about pulling apart the American-led rules-based international order by withdrawing from the Trans-Pacific Partnership (TPP), a free trade initiative that the Democratic administration of his predecessor, Barack Obama, had negotiated. That assault continued until the very end of his presidency: just days after the presidential election in 2020, Trump attempted an end run around his own national security officials by signing a rogue memorandum ordering an immediate withdrawal of all U.S. troops from Somalia and Afghanistan in order to precipitate a crisis for the new president. These initiatives bookended four years of idiosyncratic foreign policy that had hugely negative impacts on all friends and allies of the United States, and on the American world itself.

It is true that the assault on the American world from within was slowed by the election of Joe Biden in 2020. But the patterns of American politics in the next several years will determine the broad direction of American foreign policy — and thus the future of the American world. Chapter 3 examines contemporary politics in the United States, particularly the internal politics of the Republican Party and the enduring legacies of the Trump presidency. The broader political movement that Trump mobilized remains a potent force in American politics. More importantly, the Republican Party remains at its core an anti-democratic, illiberal, and authoritarian political party, and that will have a significant impact on American foreign policy in the years ahead.

In Chapter 4, we look at the likely shifts in American foreign policy in the future, particularly if conservative-nationalist trends reassert themselves. A conservative-nationalist Republican administration is likely to have learned some lessons from Trump's presidency, in particular how his conservative-nationalist foreign policy was slowed and skewed by so many so-called adults in the room who tried to erect guardrails against his crazier foreign policy proclivities.[3] But even if the next Republican president does not regard the American bureaucracy as Trump did — as the "deep state," a clandestine and powerful group of government officials conniving to thwart his presidency — it is likely that he or she will take steps to blunt the policy impact of the bureaucracy by resurrecting measures that Trump introduced late in his presidency and that were then immediately reversed by the Biden administration. Chapter 4 will also sketch out how global politics is likely to unfold under another conservative-nationalist president, focusing on what is likely to happen in Europe and in the western Pacific.

If a renewal of the assault from within by an America First administration is added to the ongoing twin assaults on the American world from Russia and China, we are likely to see the end of the American world as we have known it. Chapter 5 explores the arrival instead of a new era, which we might name by resurrecting a term coined by political commentator Fareed Zakaria a decade and a half ago: the "post-American world."[4] But this post-American era will, however, not be the world envisaged by Zakaria in 2008. In that world, the shift in global power marked by the "rise of the rest" relative to the American-led West was what created the post-American world; in Zakaria's portrait, the United States was still very much a global leader and the West still very much a force in global politics. By contrast, the post-American world that is likely to emerge in the

2020s will be marked not only by the absence of American leadership, but also by the fracturing of the West as a relatively unified geostrategic force in global politics.

In Chapter 6 we explore the implications for Canadians of the persistence of America First ideas in the United States, and the likely difficulties that we will have in navigating this new world. It suggests that in the next decade, the world that Canada will have to deal with will look increasingly like the world that Canadians dealt with in the decade before the outbreak of the First World War in 1914: a multipolar array of great powers and a world in which the United States did not have the kind of leadership role that it embraced during and after the Second World War.

The world will look different for Canadians in one important respect. In the early 1900s, Canada was on its own with its American neighbour, but this solitude was mitigated by Canada's membership in the British Empire. If the West fragments in the 2020s as a result of the purposeful abandonment of global leadership by the United States, there will no longer be those connections across the Atlantic, the Pacific, and the Arctic circumpolar region that Canada has always had in the past eighty years to ease the challenges of being geostrategically all alone with the Americans in North America.

Navigating a world in which the United States has abandoned its leadership role in global politics will be particularly difficult for Canadians. The political dysfunctions in the United States itself will have a northward impact, reshaping politics in this country in the process. The end of the American world will also have a significant impact on the well-being of Canadians. Without the American-led rules-based global trading order that undergirded and promoted globalization in the late twentieth century, Canadians will be completely at the mercy of an always-protectionist United States. Most importantly, an America that is disconnected from friends and allies in Europe and the western Pacific, and increasingly focused on

great-power competition, is likely to become increasingly belligerent in global politics. In such circumstances, systemic war becomes
more likely. We conclude by looking at what the Canadian government might do to prepare for the possibility of the arrival of a post-
American world — and for the possibility that Canada will be, for
the first time in its modern history, alone in the world.

1.

CANADA'S AMERICAN WORLD

The world that Canadians have lived in for the last eighty years is often described as the *American* world, reflecting the degree to which the United States has played a central role in global politics since Americans ended twenty years of isolation after the Japanese attack on Pearl Harbor in December 1941. Sometimes the international order that came into being following the Second World War is described as "liberal," but we need to recognize that the liberal order helped keep many illiberal, authoritarian, and abusive regimes in power.[1] And while we often speak in the singular about the postwar international order, there were in fact various iterations of the global order that evolved over the decades of the Cold War and the post–Cold War eras. However, as political scientist John Ikenberry notes, there was one commonality in all those iterations: they were "organized around economic openness, multilateral institutions, security cooperation and democratic solidarity."[2] And all of the iterations of the international order since 1945 were maintained by the huge wealth, the industrial and technical capacity, the massive military capability, and the cultural and ideological dominance of the United States.

But that American world was also a result of leadership. U.S. presidents — backed by Congress and, ultimately, American voters — were consistently willing to use the superordinate power of the United States to shape the global order. While that order was unabashedly designed to protect and advance parochial American interests, American leaders always worked hard to ensure that it had the approval of a worldwide network of friends and allies, successfully convincing them that what was good for the United States was good for them, too. The commitment to asserting global leadership was a constant in American politics between 1941 and 2016: all thirteen presidents during that era — seven Democrats and six Republicans — were committed to this approach (even if their particular policies may have varied).

The American World and the West

One of the consequences of that leadership was that the American world was also a *Western* world. For there has always been an intimate relationship between the various iterations of the American-led global order and other states of the West. But what, precisely, is "the West"? We need to be able to identify the West because it is such an intimate part of the American world.

Because it is so widely used, we tend to take "the West" for granted. It is a vague and sometimes deeply problematic[3] way of conceptualizing a particular group of states. There is no widely agreed-upon definition of what it actually is, or who is "in" it, much less how one actually determines membership. Part of the problem is that the word itself is highly ambiguous. Because it has a purely geographic meaning in common parlance, it is not always clear that in International Relations the West (with a capital "W") is generally *not* a geographic term. Usage has also changed over time: during the Cold War, West and East were used as shorthand to capture the ideological division between capitalist and communist states, a binary that lost its meaning after the collapse of the Union of Soviet Socialist Republics (USSR) or Soviet Union. Today, more often than not, the West is just used without further definition or explanation.

But while we can readily agree with political scientists Christopher S. Browning and Marko Lehti that "the West is a slippery concept,"[4] it nonetheless remains an important category in contemporary world politics. For there is indeed a group of countries today that constitute what might be thought of as the "geostrategic West": these are countries that share not only certain objective commonalities, but also common geostrategic goals in global politics. Identifying the members of the geostrategic West is crucial for determining who is benefitting from the contemporary global order; knowing who is part of the West is equally crucial for determining whether that country will be protected from others in the international system.

Who constitutes the geostrategic West? Browning and Lehti argue that the usual method used to identify the West — by trying to identify objective criteria, such as "cultural, social, political, spiritual, philosophical and economic" indicators, that supposedly make a country Western — is a dead end. Rather, they suggest that we can only understand the West as an "intersubjectively framed concept." In other words, being a country of the West depends not only on meeting certain *objective* criteria, such as economic or political indicators; it also depends on *subjective* criteria, such as whether one identifies as a state of the West; and *intersubjective* criteria — whether one is also regarded as a Western country by others. If we use the approach suggested by Browning and Lehti, countries of the West may be identified by two empirical criteria — income and the degree to which a state is liberal-democratic — and one intersubjective criterion that asks: which of those states that are both high-income and high-ranking liberal democracies consider themselves, and are considered by others, to be part of the West?

Using these three criteria, we can readily identify the geostrategic West in contemporary global politics. We begin with all the members of the North Atlantic Treaty Organization (NATO), even though five members are not high-income countries (Albania, Bulgaria, Montenegro, North Macedonia, and Türkiye), and even though some NATO members are not as robustly committed to liberal-democratic principles and practices as others.[5] To this group we might add other western European countries that are high-income liberal democracies (Austria, Ireland, and Switzerland, among others). While these countries are not members of the North Atlantic alliance, they nonetheless share broad geostrategic interests with their NATO neighbours.

The geostrategic West also includes countries outside the North Atlantic area: Israel in the Middle East,[6] and Aotearoa New Zealand, Australia, the Republic of Korea, and Japan in the western Pacific. Some would include Taiwan as a country of the West.[7] Certainly, Taiwan meets the high-income and full-democracy criteria: it is an advanced high-income economy; the Economist Intelligence Unit (EIU) determined that its "democracy index" score in 2021 was 8.99, eighth highest in the world; and Freedom House, a non-profit research and advocacy organization funded by the U.S. government, gives the country a score of 94 percent. Taiwan is also an essential part of the West's geostrategic arrangements in the western Pacific, since it occupies a crucial strategic location and its economy, particularly its capacity in semiconductors, is equally strategically important to the interests of other Western states. But the intersubjective criterion remains uncertain: while many Taiwanese might consider their country to be part of the West, do other Western states consider Taiwan a country of the

West? We actually do not know, since Western governments maintain a policy of purposeful "strategic ambiguity" toward Taiwan
as part of their "one-China" policy.[8] In other words, no Western
state formally recognizes the government in Taipei as the government of the "Republic of China"; rather, most Western governments
merely "take note" of the claim by the People's Republic of China
that Taiwan is a province of China, even though the government
in Beijing has no authority there. However, twenty-nine Western
states do maintain what are known as "unofficial" relations with
Taiwan, usually conducted through trade offices in Taipei that are
not considered formal diplomatic channels. In addition, the United
States also provides defensive arms to Taiwan under the Taiwan
Relations Act of 1979. The government in Beijing tolerates this,
as does the government in Taipei, which has carefully chosen not
to declare itself de jure what it is de facto: the independent state of
Taiwan. Because this strategic ambiguity is nurtured by all sides,
we would only learn if Taiwan was really regarded as a country of
the West if the government in Beijing decided to change the status
quo, and try to eliminate Taiwan's ambiguous status, for example
by using coercion or force against it. The response by other Western
states to such a change would reveal whether they regarded Taiwan
as part of the geostrategic West.

Identifying the geostrategic West is important because, as a
whole, this group of countries has a massive population, size, productive capability, wealth, and military power. However, while we
often talk of the West in the singular, it bears stressing that it is not
at all a unitary political actor in world politics. The West compris-
es almost fifty sovereign states, each of them eager to guard their
parochial authority; and many more communities of citizens fired
to a greater or lesser degree with a nationalist desire for autonomy.
Nonetheless, there has been an essential unity in this group of states
on several key geostrategic issues. One has been a general agreement

on the broad need for a rules-based order to ensure predictability, and broad agreement on the various iterations of the international order as it evolved over time. Another has been a general acknowledgement of the leadership role of the United States in that rules-based order.

This is not to suggest that all the other governments of the West simply followed the United States blindly on every issue. Nor is it to suggest that every government was always happy with the United States or American leadership, or that the citizens in these Western countries were always comfortable with their geostrategic location as a second-tier follower. On any given issue, the United States will invariably encounter resistance and opposition from its Western friends and allies. Likewise, anti-Americanism is a common feature of the politics in many Western states.[9] Many in the West see the American world as little more than an American empire, and chafe at how much subservience by their own leaders to the United States circumscribes their nation's autonomy. Certainly, few citizens in other Western countries buy into a conceited theory invented by American International Relations scholars to explain American global leadership: hegemonic stability theory. According to this theory, the United States, by using its huge wealth and power to create global stability, was selflessly providing the world with public goods that all could benefit from and enjoy.[10]

Rather, it is to suggest that over a period of nearly eight decades, not one of the nearly fifty states that were — or became — part of the West sought to *fully* shift its geostrategic location by rejecting American leadership; renouncing its Western membership; or embracing an alternative world order articulated by another power. The "fully" is crucial, for some might argue that Türkiye under President Recep Tayyip Erdoğan has not been a model member of the West. Since the *Adalet ve Kalkınma Partisi* (Justice and Development Party, or AKP) came to power in 2002, there has been a growing drift away from the West, both geostrategically and in domestic political practice. Shifts in the AKP's foreign policy, marked by an increased willingness to partner with China and the Russian Federation, represent what political scientists Mustafa Kutlay and Ziya Öniş have called a "creeping crisis in relations with the West."[11] Türkiye has also drifted away from the liberal-democratic norms and practices found elsewhere in the Western world. It is the only Western country rated as "not free" by Freedom House, and the only "hybrid regime" in the EIU's "democracy index."[12] However, for all of this drift, Türkiye nonetheless remains very much a part of the West institutionally. It is still a member of NATO, and it still is a member of the customs union with the European Union (EU).[13] It is also a unique and unusual case: no other Western country has trod Erdoğan's path. In that sense, the American-led global order was truly hegemonic: it was dominant, widely accepted, and not challenged.

Canada, the American World, and the West

Canadians, like citizens of other Western states, embraced the American world, largely because of the significant benefits its various iterations provided them. Most important was the durable peace that their government had a small part in creating. During and after the Second World War, Canadian politicians and diplomats actively contributed to the shaping of the postwar international order, particularly pleased that the United States was not headed back into the isolationism of the interwar period.[14] Ottawa's support for the multilateral institutions created to undergird the postwar global order was driven by a widespread belief among government officials, both elected and bureaucratic, that the withdrawal of the United States from global politics after the First World War was a key contributing factor to the outbreak of the Second World War; American commitments to a new global order, they believed, would not only keep the peace but would prevent the kind of economic breakdown that had resulted in the Great Depression. As a result, Canada consistently supported the United States, even if Canada's eleven prime ministers over the years might have had different ways of expressing that commitment.

That concern helps explain why the government in Ottawa has been such an enthusiastic "joiner," eagerly helping to create, join, and support such multilateral institutions as the United Nations (UN) family of organizations, the Group of Seven (G7), the Commonwealth, and Organisation internationale de la Francophonie (OIF).[15] Canada is a member of so many international organizations, associations, coalitions, and clubs that Renato Ruggiero, the director-general of the World Trade Organization, once said that "Canadians have multilateralism in their DNA."[16] While it is a fanciful idea, it does reflect a reality about Canada's attachment to international institutions.

Canada consistently contributed military capacity to the American-led multilateral order. In addition to defending the homeland, the Canadian Armed Forces defend the continent through the North American Aerospace Defense Command (NORAD), and participate in a range of operations overseas. On seven occasions since 1964, the government in Ottawa has issued formal defence policy statements; these three roles showed up every time. The most recent paper, released by the Trudeau government in 2017, framed Canada's defence mission as "strong at home, secure in North America, and engaged in the world."[17]

That "engagement in the world" is deeply connected to Canada's support for the global order. In the late 1940s, the Canadian government recognized that a commitment by the United States to defend Europe would be crucial for the maintenance of the postwar order. Canada was therefore an ardent supporter of the North Atlantic alliance, and a persistent contributor to NATO during the Cold War era, stationing troops and aircraft in Europe to deter the Soviet Union from seeking to dominate western Europe. When the Soviet Union collapsed, NATO reinvented itself. It expanded eastward, accepting many of the states that had been dominated by the Soviet Union. It engaged in "out of area" missions. NATO deployed in the Balkans after the collapse of Yugoslavia, in Afghanistan after the terrorist attacks of September 11, 2001, in Libya in 2011, and in counter-piracy operations in the Gulf of Aden and the Indian Ocean. Canada contributed to all of these missions.

During the Cold War, Canada also contributed troops to peacekeeping missions that were designed to prevent regional conflicts from escalating into a wider war — that, at least, was the theory. When the great powers negotiated an end to the war in Indochina in 1954, Canada, along with India and Poland, sent troops to supervise the ceasefire. During the 1956 Suez crisis, Canada's foreign minister, Lester B. Pearson, worked with the United States at the United Nations to find a face-saving way for the United Kingdom and France to withdraw, thus resolving a deep split in the North Atlantic alliance. The UN force deployed to the Middle East entrenched Canada's long and deep involvement in UN peacekeeping with Canada contributing to every UN mission during the Cold War era. During the post–Cold War era, when demands for traditional peacekeeping declined, Canada contributed to multinational missions in East Timor, against the Islamic State in the Middle East, and in Mali. In addition, the Royal Canadian Navy contributed to operations with Canada's allies and partners in the Indo-Pacific region. Finally, Canada, along with Australia, New Zealand, the United Kingdom, and the United States, is a member of an intelligence alliance — the Five Eyes (FVEY).

Canadians also benefitted from the increased wealth that resulted from a key aspect of the liberal international order — the evolution of a rules-based global trading regime. Again drawing on the lessons of the 1930s, those who shaped the post-1945 order sought to expand international trade by reducing tariff barriers and eliminating protectionist non-tariff barriers. The creation of the World Trade Organization (WTO) in 1995 was the high point in this institutionalization, and occurred at the same time as technological innovations lowered transaction costs and accelerated the growth of globalization. The result was a massive increase in global trade — and a comparable increase in global wealth.

Canadian trade after 1945 became increasingly focused on the United States as the Canadian and American economies grew more integrated. As Canada grew more dependent on access to the American market, however, Canadians had to deal with the protectionism that has been a persistent feature of American politics throughout its history. Since efforts by the United States to protect its domestic markets by limiting imports invariably hurt Canadian interests, Canadians were particularly interested in how an institutionalized rules-based approach to global trade could be used to constrain American protectionist impulses. A rules-based regime for trade in North America slowly evolved over the second half of the twentieth century. It began with the willingness of the United States to sign a limited free trade agreement with Canada in defence products beginning in 1956, and then another limited free trade agreement in automobiles and auto parts in 1965. The rise of protectionist sentiment in the United States during the recession of 1981–82 prompted the Progressive Conservative government of Brian Mulroney to initiate comprehensive free trade negotiations with the administration of Ronald Reagan. A bilateral free trade agreement was signed in January 1988. In 1991 the United States and Mexico began free trade talks, which were then trilateralized to include Canada, resulting in the North American Free Trade Agreement (NAFTA) that came into force on January 1, 1994. In the post–Cold War era, Canadian governments, both Liberal and Conservative, sought to expand rules-based trade agreements, both bilateral and multilateral. Canada participated in the efforts to create a Free Trade Area of the Americas, and was part of the Trans-Pacific Partnership. As the government in Ottawa loves to point out, Canada is the only G7 country that has comprehensive free trade arrangements with all its members.

There can be little doubt that over the last eighty years, Canadians have benefitted considerably from being part of the American world. The superordinate military power of the United States, and in particular its vastly destructive nuclear arsenal, was a key factor in ensuring that the great powers did not go to war against each other during this period. To be sure, great-power systemic peace did not mean that the Cold War and post–Cold War eras were peaceful; millions of people died as a result of local wars, often instigated by the great powers themselves. But large swaths of the world, including Canada, have not experienced war on their soil since 1945. That systemic peace, when combined with the processes of globalization, produced massive increases in global wealth and improvements in living conditions.

In addition, Canadians have hugely benefitted from access to the highly protected American market. Canadian wealth increased dramatically after the Auto Pact, then CUSFTA, and then NAFTA came into force. Moreover, Canadians benefitted from the essential geostrategic safety provided by their country's geographic location and the U.S. security umbrella. Since 1945 Canadians have been in the luxurious position of not having to devote as much of their wealth to defence as those in more dangerous neighbourhoods. As political scientist Joel Sokolsky has argued, Canadians are not so much free riders as they are "easy riders": they feel comfortable spending just enough on defence to stop the United States from complaining.[18]

The American world was also a multilateralist world. The willingness of the United States to multilateralize global problems — rather than insist on trying to manage global politics with other great powers while excluding the "non-great powers" from having a "seat at the table" — was unusual in world history. For the first time, all smaller countries were given an opportunity to contribute to the management of global politics by participating in the wide variety of international organizations that operated as part of the American-led international order. For Canadians, the multilateral nature of the global order offered a range of benefits. Having a large number of global and regional institutions provided Canadians with an opportunity to work with other like-minded governments to help shape the global order, bringing a particular Canadian perspective to global problems. Without that "seat at the table," John Humphrey, a Canadian diplomat, would not have had the impact he did on the drafting of the Universal Declaration of Human Rights in 1948; Lester B. Pearson, then Canada's foreign minister, would not have been in a position to contribute to the creation of United Nations peacekeeping in 1956; Prime Minister Brian Mulroney would not have been able to contribute to the successful international protocol in 1987 that led to the repair of the ozone hole; and Lloyd Axworthy, foreign minister in Jean Chrétien's Liberal government, would not have been able to achieve a global ban on anti-personnel land mines in 1997. For Canadian leaders themselves, operating on a global stage also had domestic electoral benefits, since Canadian voters rewarded political leaders who raised Canada's global profile by bringing a Canadian perspective to global problems. The benefits of not having to be all alone in global politics, but being able to work with other states in international groups is why, for Canadians, "clubs are trump."[19]

One telling measure of the general satisfaction of Canadians with the American-led rules-based international order is the persistent dominance of political parties in Canada that were committed to supporting that order. In the twenty-five federal general elections between 1945 and 2021, the only major political party that was consistently critical of Canada's role in the American world, the Co-operative Commonwealth Federation (CCF) and its successor, the New Democratic Party (NDP), never secured enough support to form government. The two parties that did form government during this period — the Liberal Party of Canada and the different iterations of the Conservative party — were both generally supportive of the American-led global order.

The Paradox of Canada's American World

There is, however, a paradox at the heart of the persistent Canadian embrace of the American world. While Canadians consistently supported that global order, they never talk about their country as being part of an "American world." In the past some Canadians might have talked about *Pax Americana*, but this was a term more common during the Cold War era and is now increasingly out of fashion as a way to describe the "peace" that American power created for some in the global system. Today, Canadians are more likely to conceive of their country's identity in world politics as one of the Western democracies, aligned with European countries and the democracies of the western Pacific.

This conception can be best seen in the common tendency of Canadian politicians to engage in a fanciful transoceanic projection. Historically, Canada has always seen itself as an "Atlantic" country. In 1970 the government of Pierre Elliott Trudeau proclaimed that "Canada is a Pacific nation,"[20] and every government

since has made this claim. Then the Arctic was added to the transoceanic mix, so that by 2012, when Ed Fast, minister of international trade in the Conservative government of Stephen Harper,
said that "Canada is an Atlantic nation. We are a Pacific nation.
And we're also an Arctic nation," he was embracing a well-worn
trope that continues to be widely used.[21] Well might Michael Hart,
a former Canadian trade official, complain that "Canadians have
made a cult out of … seeking to be … anything but what we are, a
nation of the Americas."[22]

Moreover, when Canadians conceive of the world that their
country operates in, they tend not to see the United States in a positive light. Over the past forty years, Canadian opinion of the United
States has grown increasingly unfavourable. "Unfavourability" ratings rose from 14 percent in 1982 to 53 percent in 2017, and then
jumped to 66 percent by 2020. In the same period, "favourability"
ratings dropped from 72 percent to 44 percent, and to just 20 percent in 2020. Two years later, after the departure of Trump, the
favourability rating had recovered, but only to 43 percent.[23]

Now, it is true that in every poll that measures Canadian attitudes toward the United States, the results depend heavily on
the popularity in Canada of the American president at the time.
During the presidencies of George W. Bush and Donald J. Trump,
both of whom were highly unpopular among Canadians, negative
opinions of the United States intensified. By contrast, favourability
ratings jumped dramatically when Barack Obama, who was exceedingly popular in Canada, came to office. Joe Biden is less popular
than Obama was, but we can still see the same shift in Canadian
attitudes in 2021 and 2022. That relationship is particularly evident
when Canadians are asked whether they have confidence in the
president "to do the right thing regarding world affairs": the secu-
lar trend line slopes down during the Bush years to the high 20s,
then soars into the high 80s during the Obama presidency, plunges

again during the Trump era, this time to the low 20s, and jumps back to the high 70s when Biden takes over. (It should be noted that Canadians are by no means alone in their radically changing confidence in American presidents: the same peaks and valleys are also evident in European views of these presidents.)[24]

However, even if Canadian favourability and confidence scores tend to rise and fall sharply depending on who is in the White House, there is one persistent belief that has tended to remain relatively unchanged over the last decade and a half. Significant numbers of Canadians see the United States as a "negative force" in the world: 52 percent in 2008, 58 percent in 2018, and 46 percent in 2022.[25]

It might seem odd that Canadians who have been so comfortable with being an integral part of the "American world" would hold such a persistently negative view of the role of the United States in global politics. This contradiction can in part be explained by looking at how Canadians have been encouraged by their political leaders to look at the United States in world affairs. In the post–Cold War era, for example, the Liberal governments of Jean Chrétien (1993–2003) and Paul Martin (2003–2006) were particularly critical of the exercise of American global power. Lloyd Axworthy, the foreign minister from 1996 to 2000, reflected this essentially negative view in a book written after he retired. Canadians, he wrote, should have no interest in associating themselves with "the way of the warrior, using the immense reach of a military apparatus to seduce, shape and when necessary coerce compliance with its own set of goals, values and interests, increasingly disdainful of any international rules of restraint."[26] Axworthy did not name the country he was talking about — but he didn't have to, for there was only one state that fit that description. However, Axworthy was reflecting on a broader dynamic during this era: the willingness of Liberal ministers to distance Canada from American global power, often for electoral purposes.[27]

On the other hand, while there were many pro-American politicians in Ottawa — including some of Chrétien's and Martin's own MPs — one simply cannot find a speech by a minister during this era that celebrated the benefits to Canadians of the American-led rules-based international order, not even after the Conservative Party of Canada under Stephen Harper won the 2006 election. Under Harper the anti-Americanism that had been encouraged by the Liberals ceased. For his part Harper never made any secret of his positive view of the United States. "We are lucky to have the Americans as our neighbour, ally and friend," he had said to the House of Commons as leader of the opposition in April 2003. "It is not something for us to guard against. It is our biggest asset in this very dangerous world."[28]

It was expected that Harper's pro-American outlook would lead to closer relations, particularly since, as political scientist Duane Bratt has noted, Harper "intrinsically understood how important the U.S. was to Canada in terms of economic and investment matters, continental security, international peace and stability, and even Canada's place in the world."[29] However, Canadian-American relations grew increasingly conflictual, particularly after Barack Obama became president, and the two governments clashed over the Keystone XL pipeline. By 2015 the personal relationship between Harper and Obama had soured, Harper had postponed a leaders' summit with the United States and Mexico, and the U.S. ambassador in Ottawa, Bruce Heyman, was being given the cold shoulder by Conservative ministers.[30] In such a frosty environment, there was little inclination for Conservative ministers to sing the praises of the American-led international order.

More importantly, until 2017 there was no particular *need* to sing those praises, or to urge Canadians not to take the American world for granted. It was only when Trump was elected president that that calculation changed. Less than six months into his presidency, Chrystia Freeland, the foreign minister, stood up in the House of Commons and gave the kind of speech that Canadians had never before heard from a minister — and a Liberal minister at that. Freeland's speech was an unabashed celebration not only of the international rules-based order that had kept the peace since the end of the Second World War, but also an unprecedented celebration of the American role in its creation and maintenance.[31]

A year later, Freeland returned to these themes in another speech, this one delivered in Washington itself. Not only did she thank the Americans in her audience for their country's contributions to the international order, but she encouraged them to renew their faith in that order.[32] But Freeland's speeches, while historic, faded from view in Canada as the threat that prompted them appeared to have passed. The reality, however, was that the global order that Freeland was celebrating remained very much under assault. To an exploration of that broader assault on the American world we now turn.

2.

THE ASSAULT ON THE AMERICAN WORLD

In the last ten years, the American world that has been so central to Canadian foreign policy has been increasingly under assault from three directions. Two of the challenges come from other great powers in the international system: the increasing revanchism of the Russian Federation under President Vladimir Putin, and the increasing assertiveness of the People's Republic of China under paramount leader Xi Jinping. The third challenge is more recent, and paradoxically comes from within — from the United States itself.

The End of the Cold War: A Transformation?

With the end of the Cold War in 1991, the United States was the only great power left in global politics. The other "pole" of power in the bipolar system, the Soviet Union, was dissolved by Mikhail Gorbachev into fifteen independent states. And while the Russian Federation, the principal successor state of the Soviet Union, still had a massive nuclear arsenal, it was no longer the superpower that it had been during the Cold War, particularly as it tried to make the wrenching shift from a centrally planned to a market economy. In 1991 China was just beginning to rise, but it was not yet a global power. Its nuclear arsenal was small, its military was relatively undeveloped, its economy was still seeking to attract foreign direct investment, its population was still overwhelmingly rural, and hundreds of millions of Chinese still lived below the international poverty line.

This was what political columnist Charles Krauthammer called the "unipolar moment,"[1] a time when the United States enjoyed unchallenged dominance in global politics. The dominance — political, military, economic, technological, ideological, and cultural — turned out to be so great that Hubert Védrine, the French foreign minister from 1997 to 2002, claimed that the word we had used to describe the two great powers during the Cold War, "superpower," no longer adequately captured the vastness of American power. Rather, he suggested, the United States should be considered a "hyperpower" (*hyperpuissance*).[2] What challenges there were to American interests in the decade after the Cold War ended came from smaller countries, invariably described by American politicians as "rogue states" — Cuba, North Korea, Iraq, Iran, and Libya — or non-state actors like Al-Qaeda.

The arrival of the unipolar moment also transformed the intense rivalries of the Cold War among the three large powers. Those rivalries had evolved in different ways. The bitter bipolar rivalry between the Soviet Union and the United States varied in intensity over the course of the Cold War. The Soviet Union and China had begun the Cold War era as allies and friends, but after the death of Joseph Stalin, the friendship turned into a rivalry that grew so bitter that the two great powers eventually fought a seven-month border war in 1969. In the 1980s China began to cooperate with the West to help bring about the end of Soviet global ambitions, which marked a final stage in a relationship that evolved from war-fighting during the Korean War in the early 1950s to Cold War rivalry in the 1960s and early 1970s.

After the end of the Cold War, the Russian Federation was no longer seen as a rival by either Washington or Beijing, largely because its first president, Boris Yeltsin, and his foreign minister, Andrei Kozyrev, sought closer relations with the West. By contrast, the cooperation between China and the United States did not evolve into great-power friendship. American support for the protestors in Tiananmen Square in 1989 deeply worried the leadership in Beijing, who saw the protests as an existential threat to the continued dominance of the Communist Party of China (CPC), and thus the very existence of the party-state itself. While China's leaders had no qualms about squelching the Tiananmen protests by force, their concerns about the United States only grew when, just five months later, the Berlin Wall was breached and the edifice of the Soviet empire in Eastern Europe crumbled, followed by the end of the Soviet Union itself. But while Deng Xiaoping, China's paramount leader, increasingly saw the United States as a threat to China, he recognized that China was not yet powerful enough to challenge the United States and the military capabilities that it had displayed during the Gulf War in 1990–91. So Deng advised his successors to wait: China, he said, should just lay low, hide its growing capabilities, and bide its time until it was stronger, colloquially known in the West as China's "hide and bide" strategy.[3]

As a result, the unipolar moment not only looked as though there was only one great power, but it also looked as though the post–Cold War era would be an era in global politics without great-power rivalries. Was it possible that great-power rivalries would become a thing of the past? Krauthammer did not think so. In another version of his op-ed, he wrote that "No doubt, multipolarity will come in time. In perhaps another generation or so there will be great powers coequal with the United States, and the world will, in structure, resemble the pre–World War I era."[4]

Others were more optimistic. Richard Haass, the president of the Council on Foreign Relations, captured a common view of relations among the great powers when he testified before the United States Senate Foreign Relations Committee in May 2008. He argued that in the twenty-first century, global politics would be dominated by the challenges of globalization. "This is now a different world," he told the senators. "The fact that great-power competition and conflict is no longer the driving force of international relations has opened up the possibility of meaningful cooperation between and among the major powers of this era."[5]

In the event, Haass turned out to be both right and wrong. Globalization does present huge challenges to contemporary international politics, just as Haass predicted. But the world turned out to be not that different: rivalries between the great powers also returned. Krauthammer was also right and wrong. Other great powers did surely rise; it took less than a generation for Russia and China to begin to challenge the unipolar dominance of the United States, and the West more generally.

Putin's Revenge: Seeking a "Post-West World Order"

The full-scale Russian invasion of Ukraine in February 2022 was yet another step down a path that Vladimir Putin had been treading since he assumed the presidency in 2000: an effort to distance Russia from the West and to reassert Russia's power globally. What followed was a classic action-reaction dynamic that produced a progressive souring of relations in the decade after 2002 with Russian and Western actions producing tit-for-tat reactions on the other side. In the early 2000s Russians saw Western policies — the continued eastward expansion of NATO; the deployment of defensive weapons systems in Poland and the Czech Republic; the embrace of an explicit "freedom agenda" and support for "colour revolutions" — as intruding into what the Russian government saw as its proper sphere of influence. They also created, and reinforced, Putin's deep-seated grievances against the West.[6] At a conference in Munich in February 2007, Putin bluntly accused the United States of seeking to dominate the world. "What is a unipolar world?" he asked. "However one might embellish this term, at the end of the day it refers to one type of situation, namely one centre of authority, one centre of force, one centre of decision-making. It is [a] world in which there is one master, one sovereign."[7]

Even though the United States and other Western countries were concerned about the brutality of Moscow's ongoing anti-separatist operations in Chechnya and Russia's war against Georgia in 2008, Barack Obama sought to "reset" the relationship after he became U.S. president in 2009, but relations continued a downward slide over a number of issues, including conflicts in Libya in 2011 and Syria in 2013. Moscow was particularly angered by American claims that Putin's political party, United Russia, had rigged the 2011 elections for the State Duma, the lower house of Russia's Federal Assembly (a conclusion subsequently confirmed by the European Court of Human Rights), which prompted the Obama administration to involve itself in the 2012 Russian presidential election. Relations also deteriorated as a result of Western concerns over the frequency with which critics of Putin ended up being murdered, some on Western soil: Sergei Yushenkov in 2003; Paul Klebnikov in 2004; Alexander Litvinenko and Anna Politkovskaya in 2006; Stanislav Markelov, Anastasia Baburova, and Natalia Estemirova in 2009; and Boris Berezovsky in 2013.

The split widened when the Euromaidan protests began in Kyiv in November 2013. These protests were triggered by the decision of Ukraine's pro-Russian president, Viktor Yanukovych, to abandon plans to forge closer links with the European Union, and instead pursue a more pro-Russian policy. When the protests turned deadly in January and February 2014, Yanukovych was removed from office. In response, Putin ordered the seizure of the Ukrainian territory of Crimea, which Russia subsequently annexed. Putin also backed separatist militias in the Donbas region in eastern Ukraine that engaged in escalating attacks against Ukrainian government forces. Russia was then expelled from the G8, which returned to being the G7. Sanctions were imposed, and NATO intensified its "reassurance" measures in Central and Eastern Europe. One of the results of Russia's campaign of destabilization of Ukraine was the downing of Malaysian Airlines flight MH17 by a Russian Buk ground-to-air missile, killing all 298 passengers and crew.

Putin responded to the deterioration in relations with the West in a number of ways, including initiating a "pivot to China" and increasing Russian involvement in the Middle East. Moscow began courting right-wing and populist movements in the European Union. In 2016 Putin got his "revenge" for the American interference in the 2012 Russian election. He ordered a campaign to interfere in the presidential election with the aim of securing the defeat of Hillary Rodham Clinton and the victory of Donald Trump, who was seen to be Russia-friendly. The campaign included spreading disinformation and encouraging polarization among Americans. Russian operatives hacked the Democratic National Committee's computer network; they also successfully hacked the Gmail account of John Podesta, chair of Hillary Clinton's election campaign, and stole 20,000 pages of his emails. These were then strategically released by WikiLeaks, a website that publishes news leaks, on October 7, 2016, just one hour after the *Access Hollywood* tape that featured Trump boasting that he could "do anything" to women, including "grab them by the pussy." The interference efforts included working with members of Trump's campaign team on the so-called Mariupol plan. This was a scheme to create a Russian-backed autonomous republic in Ukraine's industrial heartland around the city of Mariupol with the ousted Yanukovych as its leader, in return for peace with Ukraine. A Hillary Clinton administration would not approve of such a scheme; but Trump was seen as more sympathetic, hence the Russian interest in helping Trump get elected.[8]

The invasion of Ukraine in 2022 triggered the deepest rupture yet in relations with the West. The attack can be seen as part of Putin's openly revanchist goal to reclaim the historic lands of "Ancient Rus" for Russia,[9] similar to the war against Georgia in 2008, the seizure of Crimea from Ukraine in 2014, the ongoing efforts to turn Belarus into a vassal state, and continuing Russian support for "frozen conflicts" in Transnistria, Artsakh (Nagorno-Karabakh), Abkhazia, and South Ossetia. But for the West, Putin's insistence on denying that Ukraine had any "real statehood," as he did in February 2022,[10] and Russia's attempted wholesale elimination of another sovereign state by force, went far beyond these other moves. For the West this was a violation of one of the most sacred rules of the contemporary international order and a threat to international security. Western governments also argued that the Russian armed forces had engaged in egregious violations of international humanitarian law by purposely bombing civilians and destroying civilian infrastructure; raping, torturing, and executing civilians in places like Bucha, Malaya Rohan, and Staryi Bykiv. Particularly problematic were efforts to "filter" the Ukrainian population in Russian-occupied areas by forcibly deporting hundreds of thousands of Ukrainians to camps in the Russian Federation in so-called filtration operations. The forced removal of over 16,000

Ukrainian children — some of whom were subsequently paraded at a pro-war rally in Russia — resulted in the International Criminal Court issuing arrest warrants for Putin and Maria Lvova-Belova, his commissioner for children's rights, in March 2023.

The West's responses included imposing a range of harsh sanctions on Russia, and funnelling increasing amounts of military aid to Ukraine, including battlefield intelligence, artillery rocket systems, and main battle tanks. On the Russian side, the Ukrainian counter-attacks that resulted in the deaths of tens of thousands of Russian soldiers, thanks in part to Western military aid, were widely painted by Russian state-controlled media and by Putin himself as a war being waged by the West against Russia.

The invasion also accelerated the increasing decoupling of the Russian economy from the West. Western sanctions produced massive disruptions in the market. As Western companies left Russia, and more than 100,000 conscription-age Russians fled to Georgia, shortages in both labour and goods began to develop. Supply chains of all sorts broke down. Even global civil aviation was affected by the closure of Russian airspace to Western aircraft. Other disruptions included the movement of Ukrainian grain to markets in the global south, and interruptions in flows of energy from Russia to Europe as Europeans moved to wean themselves from dependence on Russian energy supplies.

By 2022 the Russian assault on the American-led international order was fully apparent. Russian rejectionism had both local and global goals. The full-scale invasion of Ukraine was partly local — a larger push to restore Russian dominance over its immediate neighbourhood — but partly global. As Russia's foreign minister, Sergey Lavrov, put it explicitly in 2017, Russia was interested in creating what he called a "post-West world order." The precise nature of this order, however, was less than apparent. Certainly, Lavrov's conception included a world in which the West could no longer, as he put it, "call the shots" globally. But it is clear that the Russian conception of global order permits great powers like Russia to "call the shots" if they can. There are, Putin argued in June 2022, only two kinds of countries: sovereign countries that are strong enough to have the ability to make decisions independently and autonomously, and colonies. "There is no in-between, no intermediate state," he said. "Either a country is sovereign, or it is a colony, no matter what the colonies are called."[11] As political scientist Roland Paris has argued, this particular interpretation of sovereignty has long historical roots, but is very much at odds with the Westphalian understanding of sovereignty. Named for the Peace of Westphalia that brought the Thirty Years War to an end in 1648, Westphalian sovereignty gives every country, powerful or weak, the legal and equal right to make independent decisions for itself.[12] Putin's interpretation of sovereignty reflects most clearly the Russian rejection of the American world, which was deeply premised on a Westphalian understanding of sovereignty.

Xi's "China Dream": Playing the Long Game

Attempts by China to distance itself from the West were also underway, although the distancing had very different causes and took very different forms. When Xi Jinping became paramount leader of the Chinese party-state — he was elected general secretary of the Communist Party of China and chairman of the Central Military Commission on November 15, 2012, and then elected president on March 14, 2013 — he continued to pursue the policy of increasing assertiveness for China in global affairs that had first been embraced by his predecessor, Hu Jintao.

Under Xi, however, that assertiveness was transformed into a much broader ambition. After he became general secretary in 2012,

Xi proclaimed that the "China dream" was "the great rejuvenation of the Chinese nation" — and that rejuvenation would see China as a great power able to shape the international order. To do this, Xi embraced a new guiding doctrine for Chinese foreign policy that claimed unambiguously that China was a great power, and that it had to assert that status in international affairs — albeit with a distinctive Chinese style.[13] Under the broad umbrella of this new doctrine, the government in Beijing began to expand its global diplomatic and economic reach. It began placing more emphasis on its activities in, and support for, the United Nations and its related organizations, becoming, for example, a major contributor to UN peacekeeping. It launched the ambitious Belt and Road Initiative (BRI), a program designed to encourage Chinese investment in major infrastructure projects on a global scale; Beijing lost no time in signing cooperation agreements with 149 countries and thirty-two international organizations, complemented by nineteen free trade agreements. China also launched new international institutions like the Asian Infrastructure Investment Bank, a multilateral development bank designed to work alongside the World Bank and the Asian Development Bank.[14]

This new doctrine for asserting China's growing great-power status does have an odd-sounding official English name: "Major Country Diplomacy with Chinese Characteristics." The official translation of the Chinese name, 中国特色大国外交, takes the characters 大国 (dà guó, literally "big country"), which always translate as "great power" when used in an International Relations context, and instead embraces a term that no one would actually ever use in English. But the choice was purposeful: Beijing believed that the term "great power" was overly aggressive while "major country" was seen as more neutral,[15] an amusingly ironic explanation given how aggressive Chinese foreign policy actually became under Xi.

For China was not only more assertive in its pursuit of "Major Country Diplomacy with Chinese Characteristics." It also began to be much more belligerent, particularly when it thought that Chinese interests were being crossed. It became increasingly hypersensitive to what it regarded as Western interference in what it claimed were purely Chinese internal affairs. Western support for protestors in Hong Kong in 2014 and 2019; Western criticism of the genocidal policies the party-state adopted to deal with the rise of violent extremism in Xinjiang; Western encouragement of "splittists" in Tibet; and Western engagement with Taiwan — all were regarded as part of a larger Western campaign to undermine China and thwart its ability to return to its rightful place as one of the world's great powers.

Beijing became increasingly forceful in asserting its territorial and maritime claims. For example, China vigorously rejected the 2016 decision of the Permanent Court of Arbitration that China's expansive maritime claims in the South China Sea, based on a "nine-dash line" that had been drawn in the 1940s, lacked any basis in international law. China has created military bases on islands that it has artificially created out of rocks and reefs in the South China Sea. China's armed forces have sunk Vietnamese and Philippine fishing vessels, harassed American naval vessels, and buzzed Australian and Canadian aircraft conducting patrols in international airspace. In June 2020 forty Chinese and twenty Indian soldiers died in clashes along the contested border in the Galwan River valley.

Also indicative of this new assertiveness was the abrasive style adopted by many Chinese diplomats, known as "wolf warrior" diplomacy, after a 2017 Chinese film, *Wolf Warrior 2*, a jingoistic tale of a special forces soldier who rescues some of his friends and Chinese workers in an unnamed war-torn African nation and fights American mercenaries. The publicity poster for the film featured a tag line — "Those who offend my China will be punished, even if they are far away!"[16] — that was eagerly embraced by "wolf warrior" diplomats in Chinese embassies and consulates around the world. Many used social media to push their message: by 2020 some sixty Chinese diplomats were on Twitter, many of them adopting abusive and abrasive language in their tweets. Their combative style was explicitly endorsed by the Chinese foreign minister, Wang Yi: "We never pick a fight or bully others," Wang told a news conference in Beijing in May 2020, "but we have principles and guts. We will push back against any deliberate insult, resolutely defend our national honor and dignity."[17]

Although the government in Beijing is quick to loudly denounce what it regards as foreign interference in Chinese affairs, it has no difficulty in interfering in other countries. For example, since 2014 the Chinese Ministry of Public Security, in cooperation with the People's Liberation Army (PLA) and the Ministry of State Security, have operated a joint program, Operation Fox Hunt, to counter economic corruption by Chinese officials who move money abroad. However, many of the "foxes" hunted are overseas. A tiny number are arrested under INTERPOL "red notices" and extradited to China; the vast majority are repatriated to China covertly — much to the chagrin of foreign governments on whose territory the "hunt" takes place.[18] In 2015 Operation Fox Hunt was folded into a broader anti-corruption campaign, Sky Net, that included efforts to track down the movement of illicit money overseas and recover illegal gains from graft and fraud. Likewise, China has established over one hundred "police overseas service stations" in fifty-three countries. Known as "110 Overseas" (after China's emergency phone number), these offices are nominally intended to provide services like renewing driver's licences to Chinese citizens living abroad. However, there is considerable evidence that these "service stations" are also involved in efforts to "persuade" Chinese citizens abroad who are wanted by the authorities in China to return home (often by threatening family members still in China with sanctions such as banning children from schools, suspending medical insurance, or banning individuals from taking high-speed trains). Moreover, there is evidence that Sky Net, Fox Hunt, and 110 Overseas centres are also used for political purposes — to coerce Chinese dissidents living overseas.[19]

The People's Republic of China also tries hard to shape domestic politics in other countries so that policy outcomes will be more favourable to Chinese interests. The party-state in China has an agency — the United Front Work Department — that is specifically tasked with trying to ensure that individuals, groups, and organizations outside China, particularly in countries that have a Chinese diaspora, are supportive of Beijing's interests, and also to ensure that foreign voices critical of China or inimical to Chinese interests are cowed into silence or discredited.[20]

China's treatment of Canada and Australia provides an illustration of this assertiveness in action. The Chinese party-state has routinely interfered in domestic politics, primarily, though not exclusively, by working the sizeable Chinese diasporas in both countries. In Canada the influence efforts take a variety of forms, including election interference.[21] In November 2021 Global News reported on a series of Canadian Security Intelligence Service (CSIS) briefs outlining how the Chinese embassy in Ottawa and consulates in Toronto and Vancouver sought to interfere in recent elections, including seeking to support eleven federal election candidates in 2019, placing agents in the offices of members of parliament, and working to defeat candidates who were critical of China.[22] In Australia, as in Canada, the Chinese party-state actively involves itself in local politics: a senator had to resign after being exposed as a Chinese "agent of influence," and a community leader was arrested for violating anti-foreign interference laws.[23]

But the aggressiveness also takes the form of bullying on specific decisions that Beijing regards as harmful to its interests. For example, on December 1, 2018, the Royal Canadian Mounted Police arrested Meng Wanzhou, chief financial officer of Huawei Technologies Co. Ltd., at Vancouver International Airport on a layover between Hong Kong and Mexico City. As part of its ongoing efforts to marginalize Huawei as a global telecommunications actor because of its deep connections to the Chinese state, the U.S. government had asked Canada to arrest Meng and extradite her to the United States so that she could be put on trial for fraud. Following her arrest Chinese authorities immediately arrested two Canadian citizens who happened to be in China, and detained them for over a thousand days. This was followed in March 2019 by bans on the import of Canadian canola, beef, and pork. As part of its efforts to punish Canada, Chinese officials refused to meet with their Canadian counterparts.[24]

China's response to Australia's call for an international probe into the origins of COVID-19 in April 2020 followed a similar pattern. Beijing immediately imposed bans or tariffs on a wide range of Australian goods, including barley, beef, tourism, education, wine, cotton, coal, lobsters, copper ore, timber, and sugar. Diplomatic relations were frozen: Chinese ministers refused to take phone calls from, or meet with, their Australian counterparts. A spokesperson for the foreign ministry in Beijing castigated "the Australian side" for its "repeated wrong acts," and called on Australia to "take concrete actions to correct their mistakes." The embassy in Canberra accused the government of Scott Morrison of "poisoning bilateral relations" and issued a list of fourteen grievances that it demanded be addressed and corrected. A Chinese embassy official was blunt: "If you make China the enemy, China will be the enemy."

These two middle powers were not the only countries that accused China of bullying. Bangladesh, Belgium, Bhutan, India,

Indonesia, Lithuania, Nauru, New Zealand, Papua New Guinea, the Philippines, the Republic of Korea, Sri Lanka, Sweden, and Vietnam all felt the sting of angry responses by China for various alleged "misdeeds." The playbook is remarkably similar in each case: the Chinese ambassador warns that the country's relations with China will be "damaged" or there will be "bad consequences." And then some facet of the relationship is disrupted by the government in Beijing. Sometimes the threat is delivered without any attempt to hide the menace. When a Swedish bookseller being held in a Chinese prison was awarded a freedom of expression prize by the Swedish branch of PEN International in November 2019, the Chinese ambassador in Stockholm, Gui Congyu, immediately demanded that the award be withdrawn, warning in a radio interview that "we treat our friends with fine wine, but for our enemies we have shotguns" — a line from a well-known popular patriotic song, "My Motherland."[25] At times, the aggressiveness spiralled into violence. In August 2019, at an anti-Beijing protest in Vilnius to demonstrate solidarity with protestors in Hong Kong, a counter-protest was organized by the Chinese embassy with flags and banners delivered to the counter-protestors in embassy vehicles. Embassy staff were filmed scuffling with protestors and trying to seize their megaphones. In October 2020 Taiwan's trade office in Fiji was holding a "Double Tenth" national day reception in a Suva hotel when two officials from the Chinese embassy started taking photos and asking guests for their personal information. When a Taiwanese official asked them to leave, he was assaulted and had to be taken to hospital. In October 2022 an anti-Beijing demonstrator protesting outside the Chinese consulate in Manchester was pulled into the consulate grounds by consulate staff and beaten; when Manchester police asked China to waive the diplomatic immunity of six consulate officials, including the consul general himself, so that they could be interviewed, China quickly withdrew the six from the United Kingdom and flew them home.

Perhaps not surprisingly, this aggressiveness produced an array of policy responses in the West. Initiatives included efforts to limit the reach of Chinese firms such as Huawei into Western telecommunications infrastructure, and legislation designed to thwart Chinese interference in domestic politics or investment by Chinese state-owned enterprises in strategically important areas of the economy. There were also broader geostrategic moves. One was the reinvigoration of the Quadrilateral Security Dialogue, more commonly known as the Quad, a dialogue between Australia, India, Japan, and the United States that also features joint naval exercises. Another was the creation of AUKUS, a security partnership between Australia, the United Kingdom, and the United States that was designed to increase cooperation on military capabilities in cyber and artificial intelligence, hypersonic and counter-hypersonic weaponry, and undersea and electronic warfare. AUKUS was also designed as a mechanism to allow Australia to acquire nuclear-powered submarines.

Western attitudes toward China soured dramatically. The Pew Research Center, which has tracked attitudes toward China since 2002, released a poll in September 2022 that showed just how far views of China across the West had shifted: in fifteen of the seventeen Western states surveyed, unfavourable views of China generally replaced favourable views between 2002 and 2022. In some countries unfavourable opinion showed sharp spikes upward (and favourable opinions plunged sharply down) after Xi took office. Only in Italy and Belgium did the favourable/unfavourable lines not cross over time: in both countries majority opinion of China remained consistently unfavourable.[26]

Needless to say, in his report to the 20th Congress of the Communist Party of China in October 2022, Xi chose not to mention these aspects of China's relations with the West. On the contrary: the report asserted, without evident irony, that China opposed "interference in other countries' internal affairs" and "unilateralism, protectionism, and bullying of any kind," and that "China's international influence, appeal, and power to shape have risen markedly." Instead, Xi focused on how "major-country diplomacy with Chinese characteristics" was being pursued "on all fronts" — and with positive results. He stressed that China remained committed to build a "human community with a shared future." This code phrase is Beijing's alternative vision of an international order that asserts that prosperity and security will only be created "when all countries pursue the cause of common good, live in harmony, and engage in cooperation for mutual benefit."[27] Xi claimed that "we have improved China's overall diplomatic agenda and worked actively to build a global network of partnerships and foster a new type of international relations." China, he reported, "upholds true multilateralism, promotes greater democracy in international relations, and works to make global governance fairer and more equitable." The government in Beijing had shown China's "sense of duty as a responsible major country, actively participating in the reform and development of the global governance system." The report stressed China's "global vision" — the word "global" occurs seventy times in the document. The Belt and Road Initiative was cited as one example of that global engagement.[28]

When the 20th Congress endorsed Xi for another five-year term, it was also endorsing other crucial changes in policy that he had introduced. His reappointment underscored the continuing importance of Marxist ideology over market forces. In the 1990s and early 2000s, China's leaders expanded the role of the market and eagerly participated in the American-led international order; Xi, as former Australian prime minister Kevin Rudd reminds us, "has brought that era of pragmatic, nonideological governance to a crashing halt," replacing it with a new form of Marxist nation-alism.[29] But the 20th Congress also endorsed the continued embrace of "dual circulation" — the idea that China's economy should prioritize domestic consumption while remaining open to international investment and trade — suggesting that under Xi, China would continue to try to pull away from the West economically, pursuing what the analyst Willy Wo-Lap Lam has characterized as "quasi-Maoist, autarkist values."[30] But such a strategy was necessary, the report implied, because of the "drastic changes in the international landscape, especially external attempts to blackmail, contain, blockade, and exert maximum pressure on China" — a reference not only to the bans that the United States had placed on technology flows to China, but also to the increasing talk among Western countries of decoupling and "friend-shoring."[31]

China has an unambiguous geostrategic goal in challenging the American world by engaging in systemic rivalry with the West.[32] Rush Doshi, an analyst with the Brookings Institution, has called it China's "long game"[33] — slowly but surely disengaging from the Western-dominated global economy, and trying to displace the American-led global order with its alternative approach to the international system — "building a human community with a shared future." While Xi's global vision may sound pleasing to Western ears, there is little doubt that Beijing views the world "community" of the future as one in which China, as a great power, is very much at the centre with other, smaller countries expected to fall into line. Two years before Xi's ascent as paramount leader, Yang Jiechi, then China's foreign minister, put it bluntly, but clearly. "China is a big country," he reminded a gathering of ASEAN nations in Hanoi in July 2010, "and all other countries are small countries, and that's just a fact."[34] China under Xi continues to be guided by that dictum as Beijing strives to forge a new international order.[35]

Trump's Wrecking Ball: The Assault from Within

Trump's idiosyncratic approach to global politics radically shifted America's place and role in global politics, accurately confirming the characterization by *The Economist* of Trump as an insurgent whose foreign policy was inspired by a "demolition theory of foreign policy." On the cover of the June 7, 2018, issue of *The Economist* was a compelling image of Trump swinging on a wrecking ball, mirroring Miley Cyrus's pose for her 2013 hit "Wrecking Ball." (Trump, mercifully, was portrayed fully clothed.) It was an apt image: the wrecking ball wielded by Trump did widespread damage — to the practice of diplomacy, to America's relations with other countries, and ultimately, to the American world.

As president, Trump's personal style in diplomacy was uniquely bizarre. Stephanie Grisham, his press secretary and communications director, has described being in meetings between Trump and foreign leaders "where he would say the most bonkers things."[36] This was particularly true of his personal relations with other leaders of the West.[37] Six "bonkers" vignettes illustrate the pattern:

- On his introductory phone call with Malcolm Turnbull, the prime minister of Australia, in January 2017, Trump suddenly started yelling at Turnbull, and then abruptly hung up on him.
- At his first NATO summit in May 2017, Trump unceremoniously elbowed Duško Marković, prime minister of Montenegro, out of his way. When a Trump aide asked him afterwards why he had been so aggressive, Trump allegedly replied, "Oh, he's just a whiny punk bitch."
- In July 2018, in an interview with a British tabloid that was timed to coincide with his official visit to

the United Kingdom, Trump launched an open attack on Theresa May, the prime minister, accusing her of ignoring his advice on how to deal with the European Union. He claimed that her Brexit negotiating strategy had not only produced "very unfortunate" results, but had also jeopardized a trade deal with the United States.

- In August 2019 Trump expressed interest in buying Greenland, an autonomous country in the Kingdom of Denmark. When Mette Frederiksen, the Danish prime minister, responded by calling the idea "absurd," Trump called her response "nasty," and petulantly cancelled his state visit to Denmark that had been planned for the following month.

- In October 2019 Trump wrote a letter to the president of Türkiye, Recep Tayyip Erdoğan, urging him not to be a "fool."

Other aspects of Trump's personality affected the conduct of American foreign policy. Political scientist Daniel W. Drezner entitled his study of Trump *The Toddler-in-Chief* because so much of his evidence pointed to the conclusion that Trump "has the emotional and intellectual range of a misbehaving toddler." Drezner suggested that the president's toddler-like short attention span, his restlessness, and his rudeness would on occasion combine to produce a "diplomatic disaster" for American diplomacy. He pointed to Trump's behaviour at the 2018 NATO summit in Brussels, when the president apparently grew restless and bored during a speech being given by the German chancellor, Angela Merkel. All of a sudden, he got up in the middle of her speech, interrupted her to say what a great leader she was, and then abruptly left the room.[38]

We can see a similar pattern of Trump's toddler rudeness on the other side of the world. The Asia-Pacific is a region where summit meetings between national leaders play an unusually important role in relations between states; the standard cliché in the region, paraphrasing Woody Allen, is that 80 percent of success in Asia-Pacific diplomacy is just showing up. But in his four years in office, Trump went to just one Pacific summit. In November 2017 he participated in the annual summit between the United States and the Association of Southeast Asian Nations (ASEAN) in Pasay in the Philippines. As is always the case, the East Asia Summit (EAS), a meeting of leaders from sixteen countries around the western Pacific plus India and the United States, was scheduled immediately afterwards. But when the opening plenary of the EAS was delayed for two hours, Trump decided he couldn't be bothered to wait around, and instead ordered Air Force One to fly home immediately. It was the last Pacific summit he attended. In 2018 he sent his vice-president, Mike Pence, to represent the United States at the ASEAN and EAS summits in Singapore. In 2019 the United States was not even represented by a cabinet-level official; instead, Robert O'Brien, the national security adviser, was sent. (ASEAN leaders returned the snub by sending lower-level representatives to the United States–ASEAN summit.) In 2020 when both summits were held virtually because of the COVID-19 pandemic, neither Trump nor Pence nor any of his cabinet secretaries could find the time to log on to any of the virtual meetings; O'Brien was the highest-level American official participating, a move that yet again disdained America's allies, friends, and trading partners in the Pacific.

More important was Trump's impact on policy. In his four years in office, Trump actively sought to change United States policy on a range of issues to fit his long-standing views about America and the world. When Trump claimed in his inaugural address on January 20, 2017, that "we've made other countries rich while the wealth, strength, and confidence of our country has disappeared over the horizon,"[39] he was distilling a set of long-simmering resentments about the international system that had been consistently on display since he announced his bid for the presidency in 2015 (and, it might be noted, well before that). As Maggie Haberman of the *New York Times* noted in her biography, "Trump was plainly furious at nearly everyone in the world."[40]

One of Trump's favoured tropes was that the United States was being "raped" by others in the international system. In May 2016 he accused China of stealing from the United States — "the greatest theft in the history of the world" — and asserted that "we can't continue to allow China to rape our country." The following month, he levelled the same accusation against the Trans-Pacific Partnership, calling it "another disaster done and pushed by special interests who want to rape our country, just a continuing rape of our country. That's what it is, too. It's a harsh word: It's a rape of our country." Trump's propensity to characterize this exploitation of the United States as "rape" was extended to NATO: Miles Taylor, the senior Trump administration official who penned the insider memoir *A Warning* under the pseudonym Anonymous, noted that Trump repeatedly expressed a desire to leave NATO on the grounds that the United States was "getting raped" by other countries in the alliance.[41] Given the consistency of these views, it was little surprise that once in office Trump moved to translate them into policy. The imposition of tariffs on a range of trading partners for spurious reasons, the withdrawals from multilateral organizations and agreements, the undermining of European integration and his explicit encouragement of Brexit, and the persistent denigration of American alliances by Trump were all part of a consistent piece.

It is rare to see a great power actively ceding its power and leadership to other great powers in the international system as the Trump administration did. But that is what happened between

2017 and 2021. What can be called the Trump cession involved doing other great powers, notably the Russian Federation and the People's Republic of China, huge favours by withdrawing from multilateral diplomacy and sowing distrust among America's other friends and allies in the West about the commitment of the United States to the maintenance of its leadership role in global politics.

The cession was most evident in Trump's insistence on constantly denigrating American alliances. "I mean, what's an ally?" he dismissively asked *60 Minutes* correspondent Lesley Stahl in October 2018. But his question could also be read literally, for it was clear that the president had no idea how an alliance in international politics works. During the 2016 presidential campaign, for example, he was asked about the threats that Russia was making to the Baltic states, and whether these allies could count on the United States to come to their aid if Russia actually attacked them. Trump responded that many NATO members "aren't paying their bills," noting that "they have an obligation to make payments." When asked again if the United States would protect NATO allies, Trump responded, "Have they fulfilled their obligations to us? If they fulfill their obligations to us, the answer is yes." In an interview with Tucker Carlson on Fox News in 2018, Trump revealed that two years in the Oval Office hadn't taught him much about the core premise of Article 5 of the North Atlantic Treaty that guarantees that all members of the alliance, no matter how small, will be defended by all the other members. When Carlson asked, "Why should my son go to Montenegro to defend it from attack?" Trump responded: "I've asked the same question." Trump then expressed concern about what is known in International Relations as "entanglement theory" — the idea that major powers in alliances can be sucked into war by their smaller allies. "You know, Montenegro is a tiny country with very strong people," he continued. "They are very aggressive people. They may get aggressive, and congratulations, you're in World War III. But that's the way it was set up."[42]

Trump also always claimed that America's alliances were one-way affairs: during an election rally in August 2016, he claimed that the United States had to defend Japan, but "If we're attacked, Japan doesn't have to do anything. They can sit home and watch Sony television, OK?" a line that he reprised three years later as president. In a rambling phone interview on Fox in June 2019, he bemoaned the unfairness: "If Japan is attacked," he said, "we will fight World War III.... If we're attacked, Japan doesn't have to help us at all. They can watch it on a Sony television."

Throughout his presidency Trump also demonstrated repeatedly that he simply did not understand how the funding for the defence arrangements of the United States actually worked. Rather, he seemed to see America's alliances as little different from the kind of protection rackets that he would have been familiar with in the property development business in New York and Atlantic City with money putatively "owed" to the United States in return for American "protection." Such a view clearly animated Trump's dealings with Volodymyr Zelenskyy, president of Ukraine: as the South African journalist Brooks Spector put it, what Trump later was to call his "perfect phone call" with Zelenskyy on July 25, 2019, was in fact little more than the stereotypical threat of a mobster squeezing protection money from a victim: "Nice country you have there, it would be a shame if something happened to it..."[43] It was also evident in his threat in November 2019 to withdraw American troops from Japan and South Korea unless those countries paid the United States an additional 400 percent in compensation.

But the Trump cession did not only occur in the geostrategic realm. It was evident across virtually all areas of American foreign policy. Trump brought to the White House his idiosyncratic views on climate change, including his belief that "the concept of global warming was created by and for the Chinese in order to make U.S. manufacturing non-competitive," and his persistent assertion that bouts of cold weather showed that climate change was a "hoax." In June 2017 Trump announced that the United States would withdraw from the Paris climate accords, claiming fallaciously that the agreement imposed "draconian financial and economic burdens" on the United States and would cost the country "a vast fortune."[44]

In the area of nuclear non-proliferation, Trump withdrew the United States from the 1987 Intermediate-Range Nuclear Forces (INF) Treaty. He also withdrew from the Joint Comprehensive Plan of Action, the 2015 agreement between Iran and the P5+1+EU (the five permanent members of the United Nations Security Council, together with Germany and the European Union), that had limited Iran's nuclear activities. While Trump had not been as virulently opposed to the deal prior to his election, he eventually came to see it as a useful opportunity to further dismantle the legacy of his despised predecessor, Barack Obama. But the unilateral move, taken despite pleas from the European allies, was a further fissure in the transatlantic relationship.[45]

In the area of international trade, Trump withdrew the United States from the Trans-Pacific Partnership on his first full day in office, completely ignoring that the TPP had been an initiative to shore up American power in the Asia-Pacific. Over the course of his presidency, his administration also purposely sought to hamstring the World Trade Organization by blocking appointments to the Appellate Body, jeopardizing the dispute settlement mechanism. He openly attacked the European Union: one of his favourite lines was that "the European Union is possibly as bad as China, just smaller." He claimed, showing his ignorance of twentieth-century European history, that the EU "was formed in order to take advantage of the United States." He enthusiastically sought to subvert the EU by openly encouraging the United Kingdom to vote to leave in the Brexit referendum — and then afterwards pursued a unabashed predatory trade policy toward the U.K. The Trump administration arbitrarily imposed tariffs on major trading partners, on occasion absurdly using Section 232 of the Trade Expansion Act — a provision that allows the president to impose duties on imports that are deemed to threaten American national security — against American allies like Australia, Canada, and Korea. As political scientist Kristen Hopewell has put it, "The world's dominant power began behaving as a rogue state in the multilateral trading system."[46]

Trump also ceded ground on international human rights. In his memoirs John Bolton, Trump's national security adviser in 2018–19, revealed what many had suspected: that Trump had little interest in encouraging human rights observance, particularly in China. For example, as the thirtieth anniversary of the Tiananmen Square massacre approached in 2019, Trump refused to issue the usual commemorative statement, saying, "That was fifteen years ago. Who cares about it?" — a response that not only revealed yet another example of his lack of historical knowledge, but also his general attitude toward international human rights. At a dinner at the Group of Twenty (G20) summit in Osaka in June 2019, Xi Jinping was explaining to Trump why "vocational training centres" were needed in Xinjiang to solve the problem of Uyghur terrorism. Trump encouraged Xi to go ahead with building the camps, saying that it was "exactly the right thing to do." On the protests in Hong Kong in 2019, Trump was impressed by the size of the protests, but he didn't want the United States involved — "We have human rights problems, too."[47] According to CNN, Trump promised Xi in a phone call in June 2019 that the United States would remain silent on the Hong Kong protests while trade talks between China and the United States were underway.

The Trump cession was also evident in the realm of moral leadership that the United States has traditionally asserted in global affairs. This is most unambiguously reflected in the idea of American exceptionalism — the idea that America is different from all other states in international politics because it is a "city on a hill," and thus a moral beacon to others in the world.[48] During Trump's presidency, American claims to such moral leadership globally were ceded to others in numerous ways. The president himself proved only too happy to rubbish American city-on-a-hill pretentions. In an interview on Fox News in February 2017, Bill O'Reilly asked Trump why he would want to get along with Putin, since "Putin's a killer." Trump immediately responded: "Lot of killers. A lot of killers. What, you think our country's so innocent?"

The COVID-19 pandemic also transformed the meaning of American exceptionalism — since the United States under Trump was truly exceptional in how poorly it managed the pandemic. Despite having the world's most technically advanced health care system, and despite being the global leader in the speedy development of highly effective mRNA vaccines, the United States experienced more COVID deaths than any other country in the world, and a per-capita death rate that was three times as high as that of Canada. Incredibly, between February 2020 and March 2023, a total of 1.15 million Americans died from COVID-19. But hundreds of thousands of those deaths would not have occurred had Trump and MAGA Republicans not insisted on politicizing mask mandates, pushing spurious alternative treatments, delegitimizing vaccines when they were developed, and demonizing public health professionals such as Anthony Fauci, one of the lead members of the White House COVID task force.[49]

Likewise, the role of the United States as a leading democracy was almost entirely ceded to others during and after the Trump presidency. Certainly, in the aftermath of the 2020 elections, American claims to be a leader in democratic practice rang increasingly hollow. This was not only because the January 6th violent *auto-golpe*, or self-coup, attempt by Trump and his allies after he lost the 2020 election was a clear abandonment of core tenets of democratic practice. It is also because the eventual fate of those who planned the January 6th insurrection speaks volumes about the current commitment to democracy of Americans. Trump's coup attempt was in effect supported and legitimized by those forty-three Republicans in the Senate who voted to reject the article of impeachment against Trump for incitement of insurrection. To date, while hundreds of Trump's followers were subsequently arrested, prosecuted, and imprisoned for their role in the coup attempt, neither Trump nor any of his associates who helped him plan the *auto-golpe* — or conspired to cover up what happened on those days by, for example, deleting their texts or creating gaps in the official record — have been held accountable.[50] For its part, the Republican Party continues to actively support the former president and all of those who conspired with him to overturn the 2020 election. And tens of millions of Americans remain fundamentally unperturbed about January 6th, or about the ongoing threats to democracy posed by promoters of the lie that the 2020 election was stolen — the so-called Big Lie — or about the continuing efforts of the Republican Party to manipulate voting outcomes in future elections. Little wonder that other states, used to being lectured at by Americans in the past on their commitment to democracy, are now happy to openly reject the hectoring.

In short, Trump and his Republican enablers in the United States Congress actively ceded the power of the West to other great powers, forcing America's friends and allies to grapple with not just the evanescence of American leadership, but the dissipation of American, and thus Western, power. Importantly, Trump was completely unconcerned about American leadership. According to Gary Cohn, who served as Trump's chief economic adviser from 2017 to 2018, Trump simply had "a lack of understanding about the globe's interconnectedness and the importance of the post–World War II international order to it."[51] Steve Bannon, Trump's chief strategist during his first year as president, confirmed Trump's complete lack of commitment to the American world: "He couldn't say 'postwar rules-based international order.' It's just not the way he thinks."[52]

When Conrad Black, the newspaper publisher, columnist, and biographer, chose "a president like no other" as the subtitle for his sympathetic political biography of Trump, he clearly meant it in a positive way.[53] But Trump's uniqueness, never before experienced in contemporary global politics, not only had hugely disruptive effects on the international order, but also on all of America's friends and allies like Canada, who were forced to try to work with this "president like no other." And, of course, to wonder whether his presidency would be unique.

3.

WHITHER AMERICAN POLITICS?

When the history of our era is written, will the normalcy of the administration of Joe Biden, so welcomed by American friends and allies in 2020, turn out to be just a temporary interruption in a slow slide into a longer-term decline in American global leadership? While crystal ball–gazing is always hazardous (if not downright foolhardy), it is arguably a question on which the future of the global order hinges, and thus has significant implications for Canadians. It is also a question on which the auguries are mixed.

Did the 2022 Midterms "Break the Fever"?

The 2022 midterm election produced unexpected results. The Democratic Party was widely expected to suffer the effects of the so-called midterm curse — a loss of seats for the president's party. It was expected that the Republicans would take control of the House of Representatives and even the Senate. Fox News in particular pushed the idea that the election would be a "red wave" that would give Republicans control of both houses of Congress; Sen. Ted Cruz (R-Texas) went further, predicting the day before the election that "this is going to be not just a red wave, but a red tsunami." The wave never happened. While the Democrats did lose control of the House of Representatives, 222–213, the Republican majority was razor thin. But the Democrats not only retained control of the Senate, but actually managed to increase their Senate majority by one seat when Raphael Warner beat Herschel Walker in the Georgia runoff in December.

Equally unexpected was the fate of a number of high-profile pro-Trump candidates who went down to defeat in states and seats where Republicans were expected to do well. Candidates for the Senate who were defeated included Blake Masters in Arizona, Herschel Walker in Georgia, Adam Laxalt in Nevada, Don Bolduc in New Hampshire, and Mehmet Oz in Pennsylvania. In the House eleven Republican candidates endorsed by Trump lost, including Bo Hines in North Carolina, Sarah Palin in Alaska, and J.R. Majewski in Ohio. All were election deniers and enthusiastic supporters of Donald Trump's "Stop the Steal" campaign.[1] Some were described as extremists. For example, Majewski advocated for the abolition of "three-letter agencies" like the CIA and the FBI, and claimed to want to fight a civil war and have Republican states secede from the United States. Masters embraced an uncompromising far-right claim that the "ruling class" and "the regime" was intent on destroying America. Bolduc called New Hampshire governor Chris Sununu a "Chinese Communist sympathizer," and claimed that COVID-19 vaccines had microchips in them. Hines pledged that he would be a "MAGA warrior" committed to defunding the FBI and criminalizing abortion federally.

While much attention was focused on Congress, the 2022 midterms also determined control of state governments. One of the persistent fears in the wake of the attempted insurrection of January 6th was that a strategy similar to the one that Trump used in 2020 would be tried again in January 2025. In the aftermath of

January 6th, Republicans at the state level with support from the Republican leadership at the federal level, sought to build what journalist Barton Gellman has called "an apparatus of election theft."[2] In this view the lawsuits launched by Trump allies contesting the election and the violence on January 6th were just "sideshows." The real objective was to manipulate the Electoral College process that determines who wins presidential elections. The process for actually processing and counting Electoral College votes outlined under the U.S. Constitution and federal law is complex, and offers numerous opportunities for manipulation. In particular, because Article 2 of the Constitution gives state legislatures considerable autonomy over parts of the process, it is theoretically possible for a state legislature to abandon normal practice — which is to accept whichever slate of electors gains the most votes — and instead repudiate those results and substitute a slate of electors of its choosing. This was the essence of Trump's strategy in 2020: to ensure that in those Republican-controlled states that Biden won, the legislatures would repudiate the election results, discard the list of Biden electors, and instead approve a slate of Trump electors whose formal "certificate of votes" would be sent to Congress for counting on January 6th. In the event, Trump's plan failed because none of the Republican-controlled state legislatures being pressured by the Trump team was actually willing to take the radical step of overturning the results of the vote in their state.

However, in the months after the failure of Trump's attempt to overthrow the election, a movement emerged to make this process easier for the next election by ensuring that key positions at the state level — the governorship and the secretary of state, the office that oversees elections — would be held by loyal MAGA Republicans. This was to be achieved in the first instance by hounding nonpartisan election officials out of office, or primarying those Republican state officials who had resisted Trump's efforts to overturn the 2020 election. Another tactic was to involve the legislature in elections. A survey of twenty-five states, most, but not all, "red" states, showed that by April 2021, just three months after January 6th, 148 bills had been introduced that would take responsibility for the electoral process away from the governor and give it to the legislature. In five states, measures were introduced to criminalize or penalize decisions made by election officials, including volunteer poll workers.[3]

By May 2021 an organization had even emerged to coordinate and channel election funds to support this effort. The America First Secretary of State Coalition was a group of like-minded Republican election deniers, organized by Jim Marchant, a Nevada politician who had run for Congress in 2020. When he lost he claimed that he was a victim of election fraud, and unsuccessfully petitioned a court to order a new election. He was involved in the effort to send an alternate slate of Nevada electors to Congress to overturn the 2020 election. Marchant decided to run for secretary of state in Nevada in 2022, and was recruited by Trump to organize a coalition of MAGA Republican candidates for the secretary of state position in other states. The so-called SOS Coalition gathered fourteen candidates to seek the nomination for this position, all of whom endorsed Trump's allegations of voter fraud — and most of whom in turn were endorsed by Trump. At a Trump rally in October 2022, Marchant promised that he would "fix" the electoral system in Nevada, "And when my coalition of secretary of state candidates around the country get elected we're going to fix the whole country, and President Trump is going to be president again in 2024."

Two Republican candidates for governor were also members of the SOS Coalition: Doug Mastriano in Pennsylvania and Kari Lake in Arizona. Mastriano, a member of the Pennsylvania state senate, actively promoted the lie that Trump had lost the election; he was at the U.S. Capitol on January 6th with video showing him and his wife breaching police barricades. He was described as being Trump's "point person" in the effort to send fake electors to Washington after the 2020 election. Like Mastriano, Lake is an election denier. She won her primary by repeatedly denying that Biden was the legitimate president. She said that had she been governor in 2020, she would not have certified the Arizona results, and ran in 2022 on a platform focused on fixing elections by mandating "one-day voting," eliminating mail-in ballots and machine tabulation, instead counting paper ballots by hand.

There were other election deniers also running for governor, including Tudor Dixon in Michigan, Lee Zeldin in New York, and Tim Michels in Wisconsin. All endorsed by Trump, these candidates embraced the Big Lie. Like Mastriano and Lake, they also left no doubt that if they were elected, they would take appropriate steps to ensure that the electoral system would produce the "right" results. For example, Michels promised that as governor he would replace the bipartisan Wisconsin Elections Commission with a body composed of one representative from each of the state's heavily gerrymandered electoral districts, thus ensuring that the GOP would maintain tight control over the state elections apparatus for the next decade. His boast at a campaign stop that "Republicans will never lose another election in Wisconsin after I am elected governor" was widely interpreted by critics claiming that he was saying the quiet part out loud. While the audio clip makes it clear that he was not boasting about the likely consequences of his proposed election reforms, he could well have been, given the way that he was proposing to rig Wisconsin's electoral system.

Many of the more extreme Republican candidates at the state level went down to defeat at some stage in the electoral process. Of the fourteen SOS Coalition candidates, nine were defeated in their primaries, including Rep. Jody Hice (R-Ga.), who was attempting, with Trump's endorsement, to primary Brad Raffensperger, the

Republican secretary of state in Georgia who had openly criticized Trump for election interference. Of the five who made it to the general — Audrey Trujillo in New Mexico, Kristina Karamo in Michigan, Mark Finchem in Arizona, Diego Morales in Indiana, and Jim Marchant in Nevada — four were soundly defeated. And the only member of the Coalition who was actually elected to office in 2022, Diego Morales, a former aide to Vice-President Mike Pence, had actually denied his election denialism after he won his primary and was safely ensconced as the GOP candidate.

Finally, Republican candidates for Congress who were followers of the QAnon conspiracy did not do well in the 2022 midterms. QAnon is an anti-Semitic internet conspiracy theory and political movement whose supporters follow a mysterious individual known as Q, and believe Q's core claim that the world is controlled by a secretive cabal of satanic pedophiles and child molesters that includes Democratic politicians like Hillary Clinton and Joe Biden, Jewish financiers like George Soros, religious leaders like the Pope and the Dalai Lama, and a number of entertainers. QAnon followers believe that children are being abducted to supply a trafficking ring and tortured to extract adrenalin from their blood. QAnon adherents believe that this cabal was trying to undermine Donald Trump's presidency and thwart his (secret) efforts to defeat them. Increasing numbers of QAnon adherents started showing up at Trump's 2020 election rallies, wearing QAnon gear and waving signs with the conspiracy's signature slogan, WWG1WGA ("Where we go one, we go all"). Trump, in turn, happily sought to attract QAnon voters by amplifying QAnon social media accounts and refusing to distance himself from the conspiracy. The close connection between the QAnon and MAGA movements on the one hand, and the Republican Party on the other, was reflected in the number of members of the SOS Coalition discussed above who were QAnon followers, or the number of GOP candidates for Congress in the 2022 midterms who were on record as supporting QAnon in some way.[4] Their success rate, however, was slim. Of the forty-four Republican candidates who were on record as supporting QAnon, thirty-two of them did not survive their primaries to advance to the general in November. And of the twelve who faced voters in November, only two, Rep. Marjorie Taylor Greene (R-Ga.) and Lauren Boebert (R-Colo.), were actually elected to Congress (and by then both of them claimed that they were no longer QAnon followers).

In short, the results of the 2022 elections seem to offer some evidence that politics in the United States was turning a corner, and that the trend toward extremism and authoritarianism was coming to an end. A common metaphor was that the "fever was breaking" — with its implication that all those Republicans who had been in the grip of a sickness were finally getting better. Joe Biden was asked at a press conference the day after the election if he thought that the fever had broken. He replied that while he didn't think that the fever would break for "the super mega MAGA Republicans," he dismissed them as a "minority of the Republican Party." The next day, columnists David Brooks in the *New York Times* and Fareed Zakaria in the *Washington Post* both reached for this metaphor with a similar, positive interpretation.[5]

However, looking at the trajectory of American politics after the election, it would perhaps be more prudent to reach for another metaphor altogether. The American writer and commentator Tom Nichols suggested that we think instead of the fate of the 338,000 Allied troops who were surrounded by the Nazi German army at Dunkirk in May 1940. They were evacuated across the English Channel in a hastily organized naval operation with large numbers of little boats, mostly captained by civilian volunteers, helping out. The rescue of these forces did not eliminate the threat from Nazi Germany, but it did give the United Kingdom some breathing space. Nichols describes the midterms as "American democracy's Dunkirk": they might have been "an improvised but crucial escape from disaster" — but there was still danger ahead.[6]

After the Respite: The Dangers Ahead

Although many of the more extreme Republican candidates were defeated in the 2022 midterms, the "fever," such as it is, has by no means broken.

While the immediate threat that states controlled by "Stop the Steal" Republicans could themselves steal the next election had passed, the danger had not completely disappeared. In 2022 the United States Supreme Court agreed to hear *Moore v. Harper*, a case that focuses on the rights of state legislatures to have the final say in matters relating to federal elections. In 2021 the North Carolina Republican-dominated legislature drew new electoral maps for the state's fourteen districts, gerrymandering them so that the Republicans would always win at least ten seats. The North Carolina branch of Common Cause, a democracy watchdog, decided to take the legislature to court on the grounds that the gerrymandered districts were unconstitutional. Becky Harper, a real estate agent who was a Common Cause volunteer, offered to be listed as the lead plaintiff in the suit. In 2022 the state Supreme Court agreed with Common Cause and threw the maps out. The General Assembly, represented by its Republican Speaker, Timothy K. Moore, decided to appeal the decision to the U.S. Supreme Court, using a reading of the U.S. Constitution known as independent state legislature theory. According to this highly contentious interpretation, the Constitution gives state legislatures almost unlimited power over elections. If the Supreme Court had ruled in favour of Moore and the North Carolina General Assembly — in other words, deciding that state legislatures can run federal elections however they see fit, unencumbered by the decisions of state courts or even the state's constitution — it would have been possible for a tiny number of Republican-controlled legislatures to determine the outcomes of future elections.[7]

Second, while we saw large numbers of Republican voters in the 2022 midterms willing to cross party lines and vote against extremist candidates, there is little evidence that the intense polarization that has increasingly marked American politics since the 1990s is easing. That polarization is one of the long-term consequences of the efforts of Newt Gingrich, a Republican who represented Georgia in the House of Representatives from 1979 to 1999, and was Speaker from 1995 to 1999. Gingrich transformed Republican — and American — politics by refusing to accept the Democratic Party as legitimate opponents, avoiding any compromises with the Democrats, and generally taking a "politics-as-warfare" approach to politics in the U.S. Congress. This helped give rise to what is known as "affective polarization." Polarization in politics is most commonly based on ideological or policy differences. Affective polarization, by contrast, is based on *affect* — in other words, feelings, mood, or emotions. It focuses not only on the warm feelings one has toward members of one's own political party, but also on the negative feelings, and particularly the "othering" of those in a rival political party with "out-party hate" emerging as a stronger force than "in-party love." Affective polarization predicts that Democrats and Republicans, animated by a hatred of each other's parties, will simply vote for "their" candidates up and down the ticket — not on the basis of policy or performance, but simply on the basis of party identity and partisan animus.[8]

The third danger is the relative weakness of the Democratic Party at the state level. Over the last decade, the Democrats have had difficulty winning elections at the state and local levels. While they did better in 2022, Republicans still have more "trifectas" (states where the party controls the governorship and both houses of the state legislature) than Democrats: in 2023 there are twenty-two GOP trifectas, seventeen Democratic trifectas, and ten "divided" state governments.⁹ The failure of the Democrats to capture state legislatures is crucial. Legislatures draw Congressional district boundaries, giving Republican-dominated state legislatures a ready opportunity to gerrymander districts to Democratic disadvantage (not to mention democratic disadvantage).

The final danger comes from the degree to which the Republican Party remains in thrall to Trump and his MAGA followers. The GOP became Trump's party very quickly after he won the nomination and then the election in 2016. Many of those in the Senate Republican Conference and the House GOP Conference — the party's elected members in Congress — embraced him enthusiastically. Some, like Sen. Ted Cruz of Texas and Sen. Lindsey Graham of South Carolina, pivoted from being strident critics to ultra-loyal supporters. Some others, like Rep. Elise Stefanik of New York, appeared to adopt an "ultra-MAGA" identity as a means of advancing within the party apparatus.

Those who might have been skeptical about a president who so obviously was not a Republican in the tradition of a Ronald Reagan or a George W. Bush were cowed into obedient quiescence. Of the hundreds of Republicans elected after 2016, only a tiny number were willing to openly cross Trump: Sen. Lisa Murkowski of Alaska, Sen. Jeff Flake of Arizona, Sen. John McCain of Arizona, Rep. Adam Kinzinger of Illinois, Rep. Justin Amash of Michigan, Rep. Mark Sanford of South Carolina, Rep. William Hurd of Texas, Sen. Mitt Romney of Utah, and Rep. Liz Cheney of Wyoming.

By the time the 118th Congress began in January 2023, only Murkowski and Romney remained; all the others were either dead or had been drummed out of Congress by a party keen to purge its ranks of voices critical of Trump. Those elected Republicans who did not enthusiastically bend the knee continued to remain silent, not daring to say in public what many of them say in private, when they were happy to diss and mock Trump. Instead, they continued to look the other way, or to pretend not to have heard, or to choose not to comment, no matter how outrageous Trump's behaviour. The litany of that awful behaviour has been well rehearsed in the huge literature on the Trump years, but it bears repeating that all of that behaviour could have been brought to an end had elected Republicans chosen a different path. Instead, they supported Trump when he was impeached for abuse of power and obstruction of justice in the case of his attempt to coerce Ukraine into digging up dirt on Hunter Biden, Joe Biden's son. And they legitimized Trump's attempt at a violent self-coup on January 6th, 2021, by refusing to convict him in his second impeachment for inciting insurrection.

The usual justification offered by elected Republicans who privately opposed Trump was that standing up to Trump would mean the end of their political career.[10] They pointed to what happened to Flake and Sanford in 2018 and to those elected Republicans who committed the ultimate sin of disloyalty, voting against Trump in his second impeachment.[11] Or they pointed to what happened to Cheney and Kinzinger after they served on the House of Representatives Select Committee to Investigate the January 6th Attack on the United States Capitol. Both were censured by their local GOP party organizations, and both were subjected to death threats from Trump's MAGA supporters. Cheney was removed from her leadership position in the House and then successfully primaried; Kinzinger was essentially hounded out of Congress, choosing not to try to run again in 2022.

But for the so-called gentry GOP[12] — those Republicans who privately despised both MAGA world and its leader but were too fearful to express their loathing in public — there was a long-term and cumulative effect of many years of bending to what political scientists call the "rule of anticipated reaction," which is when you shape your behaviour on the basis of what you anticipate the result of a conflict will be. In this case, these party members remained quiet about Trump because they anticipated that if they didn't, they would be set upon by both Trump and his MAGA mob, censured by their local GOP organization, and then primaried out of Congress, their political careers in tatters. But, paradoxically, because of Trump's exceedingly thin skin that ensured that he monitored every criticism, because of the cult-like nature of his personalist MAGA world following, and because of the damage that Trump's supporters could inflict on opponents in primary politics, opposing Trump actually did not become any less difficult over time. As Jennifer Rubin of the *Washington Post* has noted, "The longer they avoid breaking with Trump, the weaker his rivals appear and the more readily he cements his position as party leader."[13]

Because there is no one left in the GOP who is willing to openly and unambiguously break with Trump, both he and his Trumpist ideas persist at the centre of American politics instead of being marginalized. Trump himself announced after the midterm election in 2022 that he would seek the presidency again, and he could easily repeat his victory in 2016, when he took advantage of the failure of the huge field of Republican candidates for president to coalesce early around another candidate. He could benefit from the highly personalist nature of his movement; his supporters are cult-like, and deeply devoted to him rather than to the Republican Party.

In addition, since 2016 MAGA Republicans have taken control of so many of the crucial Republican Party organizations at the state level, he could enjoy an unmatched advantage given so much organizing is done at the state level. He will also be able to ask all the candidates he endorsed in the 2022 midterms to provide their organizers for his on-the-ground campaign across the country.

Since the 2020 election, Trump has also demonstrated that he continues to be able to fundraise effectively. Finally, because he is so idiosyncratic, so unhinged, and so bizarre, Trump is likely to attract massive media attention, just as he did in 2016.

Moreover, Trump became the leader of the GOP in 2016, but he had no loyalty at all to the Republican Party as an institution. Trump has already threatened his party that if he does not get the nomination, he will run as an independent, take his MAGA voters with him, and severely split the GOP vote. Trump's threat to burn the party to the ground could be a potent way to bend others in the party to his will, since the GOP is eminently flammable, and every elected Republican knows it. It is for this reason that, as Jamelle Bouie of the *New York Times* put it evocatively, "Republican elites might be done with Trump, but he's not done with them."[14]

The degree to which the Republican Party remains the party of Trump can be seen in the domination of the House Republican conference by Trumpist extremists when the 118th Congress opened in 2023. Because the size of the Republican majority was so small, and Kevin McCarthy's desire to be elected Speaker so great, the hardline members of the GOP's right-wing Freedom Caucus were able to extract a variety of concessions from McCarthy. These concessions included MAGA Republicans being given important committee assignments and support for their far-right program of linking spending cuts to a government shutdown over the debt ceiling. Trump himself was involved in this process; McCarthy, after finally winning the Speakership after fifteen ballots, duly thanked Trump for exerting his influence on his behalf.

Particularly important was McCarthy's decision to make Marjorie Taylor Greene (R-Ga.) a key ally. McCarthy propelled her into a senior position in the party by giving her assignments on key committees even though she had only been in Congress for two years and had no seniority. She even began to be mentioned as

Trump's vice-presidential running mate. Greene was a QAnon follower and a conspiracy theorist. She had claimed that school shootings like Sandy Hook were staged and that no plane had hit the Pentagon on September 11, 2001. She had bruited the anti-Semitic idea that space lasers funded by a Jewish-owned bank were responsible for starting California wildfires, and repeatedly invoked the name of Jewish billionaire George Soros, a standard anti-Semitic dog whistle. She had given a speech at a White nationalist rally. Twitter had deplatformed her because she circulated disinformation about COVID-19, and the House of Representatives had voted to remove her from all committee assignments during the 117th Congress for advocating violence against Democratic politicians. She had even given everyone a good laugh in February 2022 when she revealed that she thought the Gestapo, the secret police of the Nazi Third Reich, were called the "gazpacho police."[15] But that someone with her record could rise so far in the GOP establishment is indicative of Trump's hold on the party.

Today's GOP: The Party That Trump Revealed

Paradoxically, Trump's domination of the Republican Party means that even if he is not the party's nominee, the GOP will embrace a candidate just like him — someone who is anti-democratic, authoritarian, illiberal, and racist — because that is what the party has turned into.

Its anti-democratic essence is best reflected in the willingness of the large number of elected Republicans to try to disenfranchise tens of millions of American voters on January 6th in a bid to retain power. Of the 247 elected Republicans at the end of the 116th Congress (2019–21), 147 objected to the official certification of the results of the 2020 election: eight senators and 139 representatives — 71 percent of the 195 Republicans in the House. While none of the leaders in the Senate voted with the objectors, among the House objectors were four of the eight leaders, including the minority leader, Kevin McCarthy of California, and the minority whip, Steve Scalise of Louisiana.

The GOP's anti-democratic nature is also reflected in the huge number of candidates for office in 2022 who actively propagated Trump's Big Lie. Of 1,148 Republicans seeking nomination for office tracked by FiveThirtyEight, an opinion poll analysis website, 531 partially or fully denied the 2020 election results. Of the 552 who eventually secured the GOP nomination, only 78 accepted the results of the election; 381 either fully denied the legitimacy of the election (199), raised questions about the election (61), or simply avoided answering (121). As FiveThirtyEight noted, 60 percent of Americans had an election denier on their ballots in the 2022 midterms. While some of the more extreme and high-profile deniers went down hard, overall the election deniers were markedly successful. Of the 291 denialist nominees tracked by the *Washington Post*, 179, or 63 percent, were elected.[16] At the start of the 118th Congress (2023–25), there were 156 election deniers on the GOP side, up from the 139 in 2021 who voted to object to certifying the 2020 elections. Five new Republican senators were elected in 2022, all of them election deniers, bringing the total number of serving senators who refuse to accept the 2020 election results to twelve.

The extent to which the Republican Party legitimized the Big Lie can be seen in the significant number of Republican voters who continued to believe that "Stop the Steal" is real, or that Biden was not the legitimate president, or that his win was based on fraud. More importantly, as *New York Times* writer Robert Draper has chronicled in excruciatingly sad detail, after 2020 the Republican Party as a whole became increasingly "unhinged from the truth" as it "lost its mind."[17] But the party's persistent and widely spread lies about the 2020 election have also normalized lying about important matters that are at the very heart of democratic practice. We know from those public-opinion poll results that there are tens of millions of Republican voters who do *not* believe the Big Lie; but the fact that they were nonetheless perfectly comfortable voting for candidates whom they *knew* were lying about such an important matter as the 2020 election is hugely corrosive of democratic principles. And that, in turn, has serious implications for the future of the GOP as a democratic party. The large number of election-denying Republicans in Congress and state legislatures suggests that if the opportunity for overturning a Democratic win presented itself, they would not hesitate to indulge their anti-democratic proclivities, since they know from experience that they will pay no political price at the voting booth for it.

The Republican Party's authoritarian essence can be readily seen in the degree to which it meets the standard criteria for authoritarianism. Political scientists Steven Levitsky and Daniel Ziblatt, drawing on the extensive literature on authoritarianism, provide us with what they call "behavioural warning signs" that allow us to identify an authoritarian: when a politician (1) rejects the democratic "rules of the game"; (2) denies the legitimacy of their political opponents; (3) tolerates or encourages violence as a political tool; and (4) "indicates a willingness to curtail the civil liberties of opponents, including the media."[18]

Over the course of his presidency, Trump himself provided us with repeated instances of each of these warning signs. From the outset, he rejected the most essential democratic rule — accepting the result of elections — which he maintained long after his defeat in 2020. In December 2022 he went so far as to openly call for "the termination of all rules, regulations, and articles, even those found in the Constitution," and to demand that he be declared president or new elections be held. On numerous occasions he expressed the desire to serve more than the constitutional limit of two terms in office, always claiming afterwards that it was all just a joke. He routinely accused his Democratic opponents of being "treasonous" and "un-American," claiming that they were far-left socialists intent on destroying America. He has described his critics as "human scum," a term he also applied to those investigating him for crimes.

Trump's love of violence was frequently on show: he routinely encouraged his supporters to beat up protestors at his rallies, promising them he would pay their legal bills; he approved using force against peaceful protestors; he incited his supporters to "fight like hell" on January 6th. Facing arrest and indictment in March 2023 for federal campaign finance law violations — during the 2016 election he paid $130,000 to Stormy Daniels, an adult performer, in exchange for her silence about an affair — Trump's first reaction was to encourage his supporters to "protest, take our nation back!" and to warn that his arrest would result in "death and destruction."

Likewise, Trump routinely uses the threat of arrest or jail for anyone who crosses him. From the beginning of the 2016 election campaign, he routinely painted his opponent, Hillary Rodham Clinton, as a criminal, and encouraged crowds at his rallies to chant, "Lock her up." He has called for the interrogation, arrest, and/or jailing of a wide array of public figures besides Clinton: Barack Obama; Joe Biden and his son Hunter; James Comey, former director of the FBI; Rep. Adam Schiff (D-Calif.); John Kerry, former secretary of state. He has even claimed that John Bolton, his own national security adviser in 2018–19, "should be in jail, money seized" for publishing a memoir of his time in the Trump White House. During his campaign and throughout his presidency, he routinely called the media the "enemy of the people," and has called for the jailing of the journalists who published the leaked draft of the U.S. Supreme Court decision overturning *Roe v. Wade*.[19]

But these "warning signs" were also evident in the party as a whole. The willingness of the Republicans to set aside rules and norms to maintain their power was most evident in their manipulation of Supreme Court nominations between 2016 and 2020. In 2016 the Republican majority in the Senate refused to consider Merrick Garland, who had been nominated for the Supreme Court by Barack Obama. Mitch McConnell (R-Ky.), the Majority Leader, argued that because it was an election year, the vacancy should await the election of a new president. In 2020, however, after Justice Ruth Bader Ginsberg died, the Republicans rushed through Trump's nomination of Amy Coney Barrett, shamelessly waving off the election year argument of four years earlier. She was confirmed on October 26, and received commission hours later, just a week before election day. We can also see the willingness to bend the rules to maintain power in the party's response to the discovery that one of the Republicans elected to the House of Representatives in 2022, George Santos, had manipulated the voters of New York's 3rd district by simply fabricating most of the key details about his life. However, Speaker Kevin McCarthy accepted him into the Republican Conference, worried that the razor-thin majority in the House would be threatened if Santos resigned in disgrace and a new election held.

We can see the warning signs in the GOP's embrace of political violence. The willingness of Republicans to legitimize the violent January 6th insurrection by doing nothing substantive in response to it is perhaps the clearest indication of the party's attitude toward violence as a means of maintaining political power. But there are other small but nonetheless illustrative indications that reveal where the party stands. The GOP District Committee in the 14th Congressional district in Georgia had no difficulty working to elect Marjorie Taylor Greene, even though she had advocated on a number of occasions that Nancy Pelosi, Hillary Clinton, and

Barack Obama should be executed. (Nor, clearly, did the voters of the 14th district have a problem: Greene was elected in 2020 with 74.7 percent of the vote and re-elected in 2022 with 65.9 percent.) One of Trump's own advisers, Roger Stone, who had worked on Republican campaigns since the 1970s, was recorded by a camera crew on the day before the 2020 election talking about the impending vote. "Fuck the voting," he says to an aide. "Let's get right to the violence.... We'll have to start smashing pumpkins, if you know what I mean."[20] In the 2022 midterm elections, Republican candidates in Alaska, Arizona, Florida, Maryland, Missouri, and Ohio all featured violence in their election ads. In Arizona Blake Masters, running for the Senate, claimed that the Democrats were bent on destroying America, and needed to be "stopped at any cost"; in one ad, he posed with a short-barrelled rifle that he pointedly claimed was "designed to kill people." In Missouri Eric Greitens's ad showed the candidate and a tactical team, all armed with assault rifles, storming a house, claiming to be hunting "Republicans in name only" (RINOs), urging viewers to "join the MAGA crew" and "get a RINO-hunting permit."

The illiberal nature of the contemporary Republican Party is reflected in its willingness to repudiate some of the basic tenets of liberal democracy, such as toleration and the expansion of rights. One can see this in the GOP's approach to reproductive rights. In May 2021 Governor Greg Abbott of Texas signed the Texas Heartbeat Act, designed to enforce the state's almost total ban on abortion after the detection of a fetal heartbeat by invoking a novel enforcement mechanism. Under the law state officials were prohibited from enforcing the ban, a measure designed to insulate the state government from legal challenges. Instead, citizens anywhere in the United States were given the right to sue anyone who provided a proscribed abortion — or anyone who helped a woman secure such an abortion, such as a relative or friend who advised her to have the procedure, or the taxi driver who drove her to the abortion clinic. The act directs Texas courts to award successful plaintiffs court costs and statutory damages of $10,000 for each illegal abortion.[21] In his critique of the law, David Corn of *Mother Jones* invoked *The Handmaid's Tale*,[22] arguing that the Republicans "are deputizing far-right abortion foes and egging them on to become abortion bounty hunters and informants. They are weaponizing extremists and essentially establishing an anti-abortion militia … battalions of Aunt Lydias scouring the state for abortionists and their helpmates." This, he suggested, was the "Gileadization of Texas."[23]

Likewise, a month after the Supreme Court overturned *Roe v. Wade* in its decision on *Dobbs v. Jackson Women's Health Organization* on June 24, 2022, Republicans in Congress voted against legislation introduced by the Democrats designed to ensure the right to abortion, the right to contraception, and the right to travel across state lines to seek an abortion. This was followed by an effort to codify the validity of same-sex and interracial marriage: on July 19, 2022, 157 Republicans — almost 75 percent of the GOP conference — voted against the bill. When the Respect for Marriage Act was considered by the Senate four months later, thirty-six Republican senators — the same percentage — voted against it.

The illiberal turn is also reflected in the embrace by many Republicans of Christian nationalism — the idea that the United States is essentially a Christian nation, and that good Christians should work toward "taking America back for God," to use the title of a recent scholarly work examining Christian nationalism.[24] Some Republican lawmakers, such as Rep. Marjorie Taylor Greene (R-Ga.), openly identify as Christian nationalist; in fact, Greene has sought to make the GOP the party of Christian nationalism. Some openly reject the separation of church and state enshrined in the First Amendment of the Constitution: Rep. Lauren Boebert

(R-Colo.), for example, declared in July 2022 that "I'm tired of this separation of church and state junk."

While many Republican lawmakers are more reticent than Greene and Boebert to wave their Christianity so unambiguously, there can be little doubt that the GOP remains committed to the significant number of their voters who are what the Pew Research Center calls "faith and flag conservatives." Pew identifies these voters as deeply religious Christians, socially and economically conservative, and very politically engaged. They tend to have restrictive attitudes toward abortion and same-sex marriage, and favour a robust role for religion in public life. Many believe that there is a lot of discrimination against White people in American society, and that drawing attention to the history of slavery and racism is "bad" for America. In foreign policy the vast majority of this typology group believes that military power is more effective for America than diplomacy. These voters are predominantly White; 40 percent are evangelical Christians; they are the oldest of Pew's typology groups with a mean age of fifty-seven; and overwhelmingly they are supporters of Donald Trump. While "faith and flag conservatives" might represent only 10 percent of Americans, they represent almost a quarter of those voters who identify as Republicans.[25]

Perhaps not surprisingly given the views about race held by faith-and-flag Republicans, the GOP has also established itself as the party of White racial resentment. The Republican encouragement of the struggle against putative liberal "wokeness" on matters of race, such as the performative and symbolic efforts to ban critical race theory from being taught in schools (even though it is not being taught), reflects this tendency. So does the embrace by Republicans, including those in the leadership, of the "great replacement" conspiracy theory — the racist and xenophobic idea that American demographics are being purposely changed by liberal and Democratic elites in order to disempower White

Americans by "replacing" them with immigrants, Muslims, and people of colour.

The degree to which racism is deeply embedded in the party can be seen from the reaction of elected Republicans when their leader revealed his own racism. Trump had a long record of racism going back to the early 1970s, and that racism did not disappear after he became president. When violence erupted at a "Unite the Right" rally in Charlottesville in August 2017 between anti-Semitic White supremacist protestors chanting, "Jews will not replace us" and counter-protestors, Trump treated both sides as morally equivalent, condemning "this egregious display of hatred, bigotry and violence on many sides, on many sides." At an Oval Office meeting with lawmakers in January 2018, Trump said that he wanted fewer immigrants from "shithole countries" and more from places like Norway. During the COVID-19 pandemic, he routinely called the coronavirus "kung flu" and "the Chinese virus." In July 2020 he praised the battle flag flown by the armies of the Confederate States of America in the fight to keep slavery, as a "proud symbol." In August 2020 he tried to reprise a racist birther conspiracy — his efforts to convince Americans that Barack Obama had not been born in America — by embracing a bogus claim that Kamala Harris, the Democratic vice-presidential nominee, who is Black and Asian, did not meet the citizenship requirement of the presidency. Later that month, he spoke out in defence of Kyle Rittenhouse, who had been accused of murdering two Black Lives Matter protestors in Kenosha, Wisconsin. On two occasions Trump used a racist slur to refer to Elaine Chao, a former secretary of transportation in his own cabinet and the wife of Senate Minority Leader Mitch McConnell: in October 2022 he suggested that McConnell should "seek help and advise [sic] from his China loving wife, Coco Chow!" And in January 2023, in another attack on both McConnell and Chao, he again used the racist nickname. In November 2022 he criticized the Republican governor of Virginia, Glenn Youngkin, purpose-ly misspelling it "Young Kin" and adding in parenthesis, "Sounds Chinese, doesn't it?" Later in the month, he had dinner at Mar-a-Lago with Nick Fuentes, a Holocaust-denying anti-Semitic White supremacist who founded the America First Political Action Conference. "I really like this guy," Trump was reported to have said after dinner. "He gets me!"[26]

The default Republican response to their leader's racism has been deflection, studied silence, or even just looking away ("I didn't see that comment"). The response to Trump's racist attacks on Chao was typical; Sen. Rick Scott (R-Fla.) simply shrugged it off, follow-ed by a deflection: "The president likes to give people nicknames.... I'm sure he has a nickname for me. But here's what I do know. We have to watch how we spend our money." McConnell simply said he had no comment. (Chao, by contrast, publicly lambasted Trump for his anti-Asian racism.) But the party's silence is highly strategic. In order to maintain itself as the party of White resentment, the GOP actually has very little interest in dampening racist anger and resentment among Whites. Trump's willingness to appeal to racist Americans by saying the quiet part out loud, and with a megaphone to boot, not only makes the message unambiguous, but also layers it with the legitimacy of the presidential "bully pulpit."

Perhaps the clearest indication of the anti-democratic, authori-tarian, illiberal, xenophobic, and racist tendencies in the Republican Party is the enthusiasm that Republicans demonstrate for Viktor Orbán, the prime minister of Hungary, and his successful efforts to transform Hungary under his party, Fidesz (*Fiatal Demokraták Szövetsége*, or Federation of Young Democrats), into what Orbán himself proudly characterizes as an "illiberal democracy." To build his "illiberal state," Orbán has rigged the Hungarian electoral system to ensure perpetual wins for Fidesz; extended state con-trol over much of the country's media; and appointed cronies and loyalists to judicial and civic institutions. He holds openly racist views, proclaiming, for example, in a speech in July 2022, that Europeans "should not become peoples of mixed race." In May 2022 the Conservative Political Action Conference held an overseas conference in Hungary, where Orbán spoke; CPAC then invited the prime minister to open its conference in Dallas in August, where he was welcomed and praised for his leadership. (His racist speech the month beforehand, needless to say, went unmentioned.) As Jonathan Rauch of *The Atlantic* reminds us, the Republicans see in Orbán and his achievement of "illiberal democracy" in Hungary as a model for a Trumpist return to power in Washington: "Trump has demonstrated in the United States what Orbán proved in Hungary: The public will accept authoritarianism, provided it is of the creeping variety."[27] Orbán also serves as a model at the state level in the United States, where Ron DeSantis, governor of Florida, has adopted the Fidesz playbook.

In short, if Trump does not secure the Republican nomination, it is likely that the GOP will embrace someone who fits the party's contemporary anti-democratic, authoritarian, illiberal, and racist essence. We certainly should not assume that without Trump the GOP would magically become a different party. It is true that a common view is that Trump, who had few ties to the Republican Party, was able to "hijack" the party in 2016 because the other sixteen candidates were too blinded by personal ambition to unite quickly enough around one of them in order to stop what is often characterized as Trump's "hostile takeover." According to this narrative, Trump changed the party when he became its leader with the related assumption that the party would "change back" to what it had been if he were no longer leader. Stuart Stevens, a former political operative who worked on a number of GOP campaigns at the state and presidential level, has a very different view. As he puts it succinctly, "Trump didn't *change* the Republican Party, he *revealed* it." Trump was, in short, "the logical conclusion of what the party had become."[28]

The Historical Roots of Today's GOP

Many of the attributes of today's Republican Party predate Trump. Certainly the anti-democratic nature of the Republican Party can be traced back well before 2016. For many years the GOP sought, in a variety of ways, to deal with their declining political support by reducing the number of voters, particularly non-White voters, through voter suppression and manipulating the impact of non-Republican voters through gerrymandering. Sen. Lindsey Graham of South Carolina admitted as much at the 2012 Republican National Convention. The Republicans were losing the demographics race "badly," he said. "We're not generating enough angry White guys to stay in business for the long term." Graham's "angry White guys" comment is widely quoted because it captures so well why the party has been so keen to subvert elections in the United States. The willingness of the Republicans during the Trump era to disenfranchise millions of American voters was simply the logical extension of a long-standing strategy. The party's authoritarian turn can be dated to Newt Gingrich's domination of the GOP in the 1990s. As a strategy, Gingrich's "politics-as-warfare" approach worked very well: the Republicans won a massive victory in the 1994 elections, and thereafter they never abandoned the Gingrich model. The illiberalism can be traced back to the party's embrace of evangelicals and anti-abortion activists in the 1980s. It can also be seen in the long-running and persistent strain of homophobia within the GOP, often driven by the religious beliefs of fundamentalist and conservative evangelical Christian party members. This remains particularly true at the state level, where LGBTQ+ Republicans have often been openly reviled.[29]

Finally, the GOP's contemporary racist essence has its roots in a decision made over sixty years ago. In the early 1960s, in the wake of Richard Nixon's defeat by John F. Kennedy in 1960, the Republican Party toyed with what was called the "Southern strategy" — the idea that the GOP could win the presidency by appealing to voters in the eleven southern states who were strongly opposed to the civil rights movement, desegregation, and the post-war social welfare system that provided support for Black people. In that era the Democratic Party was deeply split: Democrats in the northern and western states were generally in favour of the civil rights movement and the use of federal power to enforce the rights of Black Americans if necessary; in the South, by contrast, the Democratic Party was the home of racist White opponents of the civil rights movement. The GOP's Southern strategy proposed trying to woo these Democratic voters away by promising that a Republican administration would insist that civil rights issues would be determined at the state level. If the strategy worked, the combined Electoral College votes of these eleven states would be enough to deliver the presidency. While some elected Republicans, such as Sen. Jacob K. Javits (R-NY), presciently warned that embracing this strategy "could cost the party its very soul,"[30] the Republican candidate in the 1968 election, Richard Nixon, campaigned on a "states' rights" and "law and order" platform. In American politics these are political code words that may sound innocuous to some, but, like a dog whistle, are heard differently by others. "States' rights" is the acme of dog-whistle politics.[31] To the unattuned ear, the phrase will seem neutral; after all, who could oppose states' rights? But when racist Democrats in the South hear that the Republican Party will support states' rights, they know that it means that they can count on the GOP to oppose "liberals" imposing civil rights measures on them and using their taxes to lift the fortunes of Black Americans.

Nixon's "dog whistle" worked: in 1968 huge numbers of voters in the South abandoned the Democratic Party, giving the Electoral College votes of all the southern states except Texas to Nixon or George Wallace, a former Democratic governor of Alabama who was a committed segregationist. By 1972, when Nixon ran for re-election, the GOP won every state in the South. The appeal to racist voters continued under Ronald Reagan in the 1980s with Reagan adding code words to the dog-whistle repertoire in order to keep the White votes coming: welfare queens, forced busing, and affirmative action.

The longer-term effect of the Southern strategy, however, was to ensure that the GOP remained the party of White resentment into the 2000s and 2010s. This is reflected most clearly in how Republicans responded when a Black American was elected president in 2008. Incapable of accepting the idea of a Black family in the White House, many Republicans immediately sought to delegitimize Barack Obama by claiming that he was a Muslim, a communist, and that he was "pretending to be an American" because, it was claimed, he was not born in the United States.[32] The raw and crude racism to which Barack and Michelle Obama were subjected is a key indication of the depth of this resentment. Republicans at anti-Obama protests organized by the GOP's Tea Party movement felt quite comfortable displaying overtly racist signs; a number of Republican officials or candidates felt quite comfortable posting racist depictions of the Obamas as apes or monkeys on social media. Invariably, the response of the Republican leadership was, as usual, silence.[33] And, perhaps because of that silence, voters felt quite comfortable electing racists, as the voters of the 49th district in Kentucky did in February 2018, when they sent Dan Johnson, the Republican candidate who had posted a number of depictions of the Obamas as apes on Facebook, to the state House of Representatives, where he was welcomed into the Republican caucus.

Exploring what the Republican Party has become, and recognizing that its attributes were not created by Trump but revealed and accelerated by him, is crucial for understanding why a MAGA Republican presidency would likely bring with it a return to a Trumpist agenda, even if Trump himself is not president. We would likely see an intensification of anti-democratic moves, authoritarianism, the glorification of political violence and "strongman" leadership, illiberalism, and racism.

4.

THE PERSISTENCE OF AMERICA FIRST

When asked whom he consults on foreign policy, Donald Trump replied, "I'm speaking with myself, number one, because I have a very good brain and I've said a lot of things.... My primary consultant is myself and I have a good instinct for this stuff."[1] Perhaps this explains why American foreign policy during Trump's presidency was so shambolic and disordered, a kaleidoscope of shifting priorities and half-finished initiatives. This was partly a function of Trump's own insistence on winging it. He was a narcissistic, thin-skinned, transactional leader who was aggressively ignorant about the world and its history. He refused to read his briefing books or to take advice from experts. Instead, he depended on an overweening Dunning–Kruger confidence in his "gut instincts." The kaleidoscopic nature of American foreign policy during this period was also a function of the president's lack of discipline. "Trump lived in his own head," Bob Woodward, an investigative reporter, reminds us, "and if he wanted, out came an idea or a decision. It did not matter what anybody else thought."[2] But his ideas did not necessarily have any sustaining substance: as David Brooks of the *New York Times* so memorably put it, Trump is someone "whose thoughts are often just six fireflies beeping randomly in a jar."[3]

But there is a paradox here. On the one hand, Trump's foreign policy has not attracted much praise. More common is the assessment of Stephen M. Walt, an International Relations professor at Harvard, who concluded his final report card on American foreign policy from 2017 to 2021: "Although Trump can claim a few foreign-policy successes, his overall record is dismal."[4] Trump had promised to "Make America Great Again," a signature slogan plagiarized from Ronald Reagan's 1980 presidential election campaign. He had promised that during his presidency the United States would no longer be a global "laughing-stock." But all evidence suggests that during his presidency the role of the United States in the world was far more diminished, and the United States far less respected, than it had been before he came to power. Certainly no U.S. president has ever been openly laughed at by other world leaders as Trump was in the General Assembly of the United Nations in September 2018.[5]

And yet Trump's America First ideas continue to resonate in American politics. The protectionism and economic nationalism that Trump embraced so enthusiastically was based on a complete misunderstanding of how the global capitalist economy actually works, but it was hugely popular among Americans. Indeed, it was so popular that the Democrats, when they came to power, chose not to abandon this element of America First. Other elements of Trump's conservative-nationalist agenda, such as his criticism of multilateralism or his negative attitude toward America's allies and friends, might have been rejected by the administration of Joe Biden — and by many American voters — but we have to take into account that many Americans continue to approve of these elements of Trumpism. And we cannot ignore the longer-term implications for United States foreign policy of the fact that in the 2020 presidential elections 74,223,975 Americans looked at the Trump record and decided that they wanted another four years of Trumpism.

Both the size of that number and the hold that Trumpism continues to have on the GOP suggests that we should expect that any Republican who wins the party's nomination will pursue an America First agenda in foreign policy if elected president.

The Return of America First

Before outlining what an America First foreign policy would look like if a conservative-nationalist president returns to the White House, we need to look at why a return of an America First agenda is likely to be more effective, have a greater impact, and be more durable, than it was between 2017 and 2021. The reason is that anyone who lands the Republican nomination — even Trump himself — will have learned lessons from his foreign policy record.

While some of the failures in foreign policy were the result of Trump's own idiosyncrasies, some of the disorder came from the official level. Not all of Trump's foreign policy and national security advisers were experienced in international affairs, in large part because Trump had ostentatiously run against the foreign policy "establishment" in Washington. Many on the Republican side of that establishment became prominent "Never Trumpers" and refused to consider working for the new administration. So, for example, Trump's first national security adviser was not someone with experience in previous Republican administrations. Instead, Trump appointed Michael Flynn, a retired general who had been let go as director of the Defense Intelligence Agency in 2014 for his chaotic management style; in his post-military life he had become a conspiracy theorist and QAnon enthusiast. Trump's deputy national security adviser, Kathleen ("K.T.") McFarland, had worked in government in the defence area, but back in the 1970s and 1980s, and was a Fox TV news pundit when she was appointed. Others, like Peter Navarro, were appointed outside their area of expertise: Navarro's remit was to advise on China policy, even though he was a professor of business whose only expertise on China was a 2007 polemic, *The Coming China Wars*. The problem with expertise was compounded by the very high rate of turnover in the national security area, which, in the words of one study, was "simply off the charts."[6]

Sometimes the disconnects in foreign policy outcomes during Trump's presidency came from the numerous officials in the White House and senior officials in executive departments who remained convinced of the importance of the American-led rules-based international order, and who helped protect America's friends and allies from the worst effects of Trump's foreign policy proclivities. These were the public servants who were just trying to do their job, fighting "invisible battles" against Trump and his inner circle, and who were widely known within the public service as "the crazies."[7]

If a Republican returns to the White House, however, it is unlikely that we will see a repetition of the problems that Trump experienced at the bureaucratic level from 2017 to 2021. First, it is likely that an America First Republican would be more prepared than the Trump team was in 2016, when, by all accounts, they were taken completely by surprise when he won. In April 2021 a "White House in waiting" was created when a number of former Trump administration officials formed a new think tank, the America First Policy Institute (AFPI). While as a 501(c)(3) non-profit organization AFPI is prohibited from partisan campaigning, it nonetheless promotes an America First agenda. It is funded by anonymous megadonors, which allowed it to dramatically expand its operations, growing from twenty employees to over 150, actively promoting the agenda in fifteen states.

Second, an America First president would come to office with a heightened sensitivity to the corrosive effects of what some in

MAGA world call the "deep state" — an ill-defined group of unnamed officials in the U.S. bureaucracy who supposedly work to advance their own policy agendas and use their bureaucratic positions to foil efforts by political leaders, like Trump, to introduce new policies that they do not like. In particular, a Republican administration would be aware how Trump's conservative-nationalist foreign policy between 2017 and 2021 was slowed, skewed, and even sometimes derailed, not only by the so-called adults in the room in Washington who tried to erect guardrails against Trump's propensity to indulge his own ideas, but by the vast American bureaucracy spread around the world.

During his presidency Trump had moved to blunt the impact of the permanent federal bureaucracy. Late in his administration — in October 2020, just before the election — he issued an executive order that created a new employment category for federal civil servants. "Schedule F" appointees would no longer be protected by the Civil Service Rules and Regulations, and thus could be removed from office. This would have allowed Trump to fill the ranks of the executive agencies with those committed to his agenda.[8] It was estimated that if Trump had been re-elected in 2020, and Schedule F had been implemented, it would have affected tens of thousands of federal civil service positions. As it turned out, Trump's Schedule F initiative had a very short life: on his third day in office, Joe Biden issued an executive order repealing it. But it is likely that a Republican president would resurrect the Schedule F regime in order to reduce the ability of the civil service to slow-roll an America First agenda. Because MAGA loyalists could be placed much deeper down in the bureaucracy, both in Washington and globally, it is likely that many of the guardrails we saw operating between 2017 and 2021 would simply disappear.

What would the substance of American foreign policy look like under a Republican conservative-nationalist president? If that president is Trump himself, American foreign policy will take a particularly idiosyncratic turn, since, as the journalists Bob Woodward and Robert Costa have noted, Trump's return to the presidency will be fueled by vengeance,[9] and it is likely that that vengeance will find its expression in a highly personalized foreign policy against those foreign leaders he believes crossed him. But it is also likely that Trump would not just resume, but would accelerate, the global wrecking-ball operation he pursued so vigorously between 2017 and 2021. And this time he would have an administration that was more prepared, and, once Schedule F was reintroduced, he would have loyalists much deeper down in the bureaucracy to carry out his America First foreign policy.

But if a Republican other than Trump takes the presidency, we should not expect much of a difference in policy. Another Republican president may not demonstrate all the idiosyncratic dysfunctions in foreign policy and statecraft that Trump did, but he or she will be the leader of a party that remains deeply wedded to key foreign policy ideas that Trump articulated so clearly and that continue to resonate so well with the party's voters. Thus, it is highly unlikely that the next Republican president would abandon the essence of Trump's approach to the world.

The resumption of an America First foreign policy would be marked by exactly the same dynamic we saw after Joe Biden took office in January 2021: a concerted effort to undo the policies of the previous administration. A Republican administration would once again withdraw the United States from the Paris climate accord and would reject a multilateral approach to climate issues. More generally, a Republican administration would seek to undo the efforts of the Biden team to strengthen the alliance relationships that Trump had damaged during his presidency.

We can also expect an America First administration to resume and then expand an attack on multilateral institutions of global governance. If the Trump presidency is any indication, it is also likely that an America First administration would look with a jaundiced eye at the wide range of summits on the annual presidential agenda, from central institutions like the G7 and G20, to regional summits like the East Asia Summit. It is also possible that the administration would step away from international institutions and organizations that it judges does not directly advance American interests, from global organizations like the World Trade Organization to smaller organizations like the Arctic Council. We should also expect that the return of America First will see a resurgence of a foreign policy animated by resentment toward foreigners for taking advantage of Americans. It is thus likely we will see a renewal and an intensification of quarrels with friends, allies, and trading partners of the United States over security, trade, and a range of global issues, such as climate change, internet governance, water scarcity, ocean governance, and food security. Likewise, a conservative-nationalist president will remain deeply skeptical of the idea of American global leadership, particularly since other countries of the West will likely continue to do what gave rise to the resentments of the America First agenda in the first place. Republicans will continue to see America's allies primarily as annoying liabilities. They will continue to be resentful that the allies are getting a "free ride" on the generosity of Americans by refusing to "pay their fair share," and by refusing to devote the same proportion of their wealth to defence that Americans do. They will see these "friends" continuing to "trade unfairly" and "rip Americans off."

Moreover, the tensions driven by material quarrels will be exacerbated by a likely increase in symbolic quarrels as citizens — and even governments — in other countries of the West openly criticize the return of an anti-democratic, authoritarian, illiberal, and racist party to power. The rise of the kind of anti-Americanism in other Western countries of the sort that we saw during both the

George W. Bush and Trump administrations will, in turn, generate highly negative reactions among Americans, particularly those in government.

But it is in American relations with the two great powers, Russia and China, that we would likely see a dramatic shift in policy that will have the most profound implications for the future of the "American world." Based on present trends, the approach of a Republican administration toward each great power is likely to be different — and likely to produce very different results in each region.

Dealing with Russia

A year after Russia intensified its efforts to eliminate Ukraine as an independent state, Republicans were clearly torn on the Russian Federation and its president, Vladimir Putin. Some recognized the threat to American and Western interests posed by Putin's efforts to drive a wedge into the North Atlantic alliance by interfering in American elections in 2016 and 2020 so that Trump, whose antipathy toward Europe is well known, would be president. Some Republicans saw Russia's attempts to cow its neighbours as a threat that should be countered by the United States. Some Republicans were generally supportive of the broad policy approach adopted by the Biden administration to the invasion of Ukraine, which was to send more than $50 billion in security assistance to Ukraine, roughly half of which is military aid, so that Ukrainian forces could blunt the Russian invasion. They supported sending American weapons systems to the Ukrainian armed forces, and they welcomed the battlefield defeats that the Ukrainian forces were able to inflict on Russian forces as a result. Some Republicans, while they supported Ukraine, did worry that the Biden administration would drag the United States into a war with Russia.

But some Republicans had a very different view. On Russian interference in American politics, they took their cues from their leader, who repeatedly dismissed all the clear evidence of interference as "fake news" and referred to it as "the Russia hoax." For some Republicans, like those Trump supporters who showed up to his rallies wearing "I'd rather be a Russian than a Democrat" T-shirts, the Russian connection was intertwined with the profound polarization in American politics. Likewise, the attitudes of some Republican voters toward Vladimir Putin aligned with Trump's own "fanboy bromance" with Putin that was so clearly on display at the summit in Helsinki in July 2018; well might former Republican California governor Arnold Schwarzenegger have mocked Trump in a video: "You stood there like a little wet noodle."[10]

Putin enjoyed extraordinary levels of support among Republicans. They appeared to like his strongman style, his White racist nationalism, his embrace of Christianity, his virulent anti-LGBTQ+ positions, and his rejection of liberals and liberalism. Certainly, the extreme right fringe embraced him. At the annual America First Political Action Conference in 2022, held in Orlando on the weekend after the Russian invasion, White supremacist Nick Fuentes asked the audience for a "round of applause for Russia," and his audience responded by enthusiastically chanting, "Putin, Putin." While the alt-right AFPAC might not be broadly representative of the Republican Party, four elected Republicans gave speeches: two members of Congress, Rep. Marjorie Taylor Greene (R-Ga.) and Rep. Paul Gosar (R-Ariz.); a Republican state senator from Arizona, Wendy Rogers; and the Republican lieutenant-governor of Idaho, Janice McGeachin. Kari Lake, the Republican candidate for governor in Arizona, was scheduled to attend the conference but did not show. So the Republican fringe is not that fringe: in a poll taken in January 2022, almost two-thirds of Republicans agreed with the proposition that Putin was a "stronger leader" than Joe Biden.

That poll also reported that those respondents who named Fox News as their prime news source were particularly favourable to Putin. This is not surprising: Tucker Carlson, formerly the cable network's most watched evening anchor, has a long record of pro-Russia and anti-Ukraine comments on air, claiming for example, that because the seizure of Crimea "has no effect on America," he was "totally fine" with it, or that he was "rooting for Russia against Ukraine."[11] By May 2022 Carlson was arguing that the war in Ukraine actually had nothing to do with Ukraine at all. Rather, in his view, the Democrats were threatening to plunge the United States into yet another "forever war," not to help Ukrainians, but simply in retaliation for Russia's involvement in the 2016 election that denied Hillary Rodham Clinton the presidency.[12]

These views of Putin and Russia had an impact on the degree of opposition in MAGA world to the support for Ukraine after the Russian invasion. Trump's initial reaction was to call the invasion "genius" and a "savvy" move. Some Republicans in Congress left little doubt that they did not support Ukraine. For example, J.D. Vance of Ohio, who was elected to the Senate in the 2022 midterm election, appeared on Steve Bannon's *War Room* just before the Russian invasion and admitted: "I gotta be honest with you, I don't really care what happens to Ukraine one way or another." After the invasion an anti-Ukraine caucus emerged in the House of Representatives. From the outset Rep. Matt Gaetz (R-Fla.) opposed aid to Ukraine: at the Conservative Political Action Committee conference held in Orlando on the weekend after the invasion, Gaetz spoke out against American assistance; by October he was claiming that "maintaining Ukraine as an international money laundering Mecca" was not worth the risk of war with Russia. Gosar declared that "Ukraine is not our ally. Russia is not our enemy." At a Trump rally in Sioux City the week before the elections, Greene, who in March had called Ukrainians neo-Nazis, pledged, to cheers from the crowd, that "under Republicans, not another penny will go to Ukraine. Our country comes first." And Rep. Kevin McCarthy (R-Calif.), at the time the House Minority Leader, warned in October 2022 that there would be "no blank check" on American aid to Ukraine should the Republicans take control of the House, a warning immediately confirmed when some members of the Republican anti-Ukraine caucus in the House of Representatives — Greene, Gaetz, Andrew Clyde (R-Ga.), Barry Moore (R-Ala.), Thomas Massie (R-Ky.), and freshly elected Cory Mills (R-Fla.) — held a press conference after the election to announce that "the days of endless cash and military materiel to Ukraine are numbered." The signals on Russia, Putin, and Ukraine being sent out by the party leader and members of Congress, and amplified in the Fox News ecosystem, clearly had an impact: by December 2022 support among Republican voters for American aid to Ukraine had fallen significantly.

It was thus not surprising that as the Russian war against Ukraine ground on, the opposition to American aid among elected Republicans in the House of Representatives grew. One indication of this was that only eighty-six of the 213 Republican Representatives showed up to hear Volodymyr Zelenskyy address Congress on December 21, 2021. Greene was among those who were not there, instead tweeting earlier in the day complaining about the size of American funding for Ukraine, claiming that foreign aid was "like the American people are raped every day at the hands of their elected leaders." For his part, Massie claimed that he wouldn't listen to a speech by a "Ukrainian lobbyist."

And when the Biden administration helped negotiate a broad NATO deal to donate powerful main battle tanks to Ukraine in January 2023, there was another round of criticism. Greene claimed that the Biden administration was "depleting our own military arsenal" by giving tanks, "while China is building its military at the fastest pace in world history." Claiming that American funds to Ukraine were being used as a "corrupt slush fund and it's just killing people," Greene called for an end to American aid: "We must stop funding Ukraine. This war needs to end." On January 26, 2023, Trump echoed not only Greene's call for an end to the war, but also a common threat by commentators on Russian state-controlled media that the United States was pushing Russia into using nuclear weapons. On Truth Social, the social media site Trump had created after he was deplatformed following the January 6th insurrection, he wrote: "FIRST COME THE TANKS, THEN COME THE NUKES. Get this crazy war ended, NOW. So easy to do." In a tweet endorsing Trump for president in February 2023, Vance took aim at the support for Ukraine: "While others want to foolishly march us into WW3 over Russia and Ukraine, Trump is the only candidate running with the courage to stand up to the corrupt bipartisan foreign policy establishment." In an interview with Fox News host Sean Hannity in March 2023, Trump suggested that he could have made a deal with Putin, allowing Russia to "take over" some parts of Ukraine — though Fox News quickly edited that claim out when they replayed the interview. Ron DeSantis, the governor of Florida who is seeking the 2024 GOP presidential nomination, also weighed in on the Ukraine issue. Responding to a request from Tucker Carlson of Fox News to all the candidates for the GOP nomination, both declared and potential, DeSantis tried to appeal to the MAGA base: "While the U.S. has many vital interests ... becom[ing] further entangled in a territorial dispute between Ukraine and Russia is not one of them." (When he was criticized by some gentry GOP senators, DeSantis tried to clarify his position, but, as political scientist Daniel W. Drezner put it, he merely sank further into incoherence.[13]) The response of what Liz Cheney has called the "Putin wing of the GOP" to the Russian invasion of Ukraine is crucial for our understanding of the *trajectory* of the party's foreign policy. The fact that so many Republicans did not disavow Trump for his embrace of the leader of a great power who is so obviously committed to the destruction of the North Atlantic alliance tells us where the party is heading on this issue. That so many Republicans had a positive view of Putin and Russia also provides us with an indication of what will be in store for transatlantic relations should a Trumpist return to the White House. And the opposition of so many elected Republicans, including their leader, to the continuation of American aid to the Ukrainian effort to expel Russian forces from Ukrainian territory suggests what lies ahead.

We know that Trump's attitudes toward NATO remained constant over time. On numerous occasions during his presidency, he had wanted to withdraw the United States from the alliance, only to be sidetracked by the "adults in the room." Instead, he had bruited a withdrawal in his second term. But after his defeat, he still maintained an anti-NATO perspective. Months after the invasion of Ukraine, Trump was still pushing his protection-racket view of the alliance, and still revealing that he continues to have no commitment to defending America's allies in Europe. In a speech to the Turning Point USA Student Action Summit in Tampa in July 2022, Trump reminded his audience that when he was president, he had threatened NATO allies that if they were attacked by Russia, he would not defend those who were not "paying their bills." As he recounted it for his audience, he told NATO leaders: "That's right, I will not come to your defence." But it is a telling indication of contemporary Republican opinion about NATO that his audience reacted to this anecdote with cheers and raucous applause. Trump got the same reaction at the CPAC conference in March 2023 when he told one of his unhinged "sir" stories:[14] this one recounted how he got an unnamed European leader to promise to send him a cheque immediately ("It'll be sent by overnight mail, sir") to cover his country's "delinquent" NATO payment in order to ensure that the United States would continue to defend his country against Russia. (After basking in the cheers and applause this tale elicited, Trump then drifted into imagining how easy it would be for Russia to destroy the new NATO headquarters building in Brussels.)[15]

The unwillingness of huge numbers of Republicans to condemn the invasion of Ukraine and the continuing popularity of Trump's anti-NATO stance come together to provide a logical trajectory for American policy under a conservative-nationalist president. An America First president is likely to continue to have the same jaundiced view of the Europeans as a bunch of unfair traders and free-riders on American beneficence, happy to allow the United States to pick up the lion's share of the assistance to Ukraine. It is unlikely that the next Republican president would be willing to see the alliance as it is presently organized as promoting American interests.

But an anti-NATO president would also be likely to have a geostrategic interest in fulfilling Trump's oft-stated assertion that "having a good relationship with Russia is a good thing, not a bad thing," particularly as it is likely that a Republican president would also be looking to ramp up confrontation with the People's Republic of China. And one way that a Republican president might move to improve relations with Moscow would be to press for an end to the war.

Trump himself believed that ending the war was "so easy to do." And Russia's war against Ukraine could readily be ended if a conservative-nationalist president accepted one of the explanations for the invasion that floated in the Republican/right-wing media ecosystem in 2022. It is true that most of those explanations were little more than warmed-over talking points copied from Russian state-run media or those who spoke for the Russian government; some required plunging down conspiracy theory rabbit holes. Among these explanations:

- Ukraine was a totalitarian state that needed to be "de-nazified";
- the invasion was the result of the Western decision to expand NATO and offer Ukraine the possibility of membership;
- the Russians wanted to stop the "corrupt Zelenskyy regime" from turning Ukraine into a money-laundering centre;
- the Russians wanted to put a stop to the efforts by George Soros and other "globalists" (often used as code by anti-Semites to mean Jews) to use the U.S. State Department and the FBI to take over Ukraine;
- the Russians needed to destroy bioweapons labs that the United States was secretly running in Ukraine;
- the invasion was incited by the Biden administration to try to bring down Putin in retaliation for what he did to Hillary Rodham Clinton in 2016.

The explanation that the Russian war against Ukraine was triggered by NATO expansion was perhaps the most common (and certainly the least loony) of these right-wing explanations. For after the Cold War, NATO did expand to the east, right to the borders of the Russian Federation; it did hold out the prospect that other countries also on Russia's borders like Ukraine and Georgia could eventually join NATO. But, the argument runs, this move backed Russia into a corner. If Ukraine joined NATO and the European Union, that would pose an existential threat to Russia, just as Putin declared. The West left Moscow no other choice: Russia just *had* to remove the government of Volodymyr Zelenskyy by force in order to protect its legitimate security interests. This general argument has been articulated most prominently by the American academic

John J. Mearsheimer. While as *explanation* the thesis is deeply problematic because it gets so much wrong (as the academic critics who keep piling on Mearsheimer at every opportunity routinely point out[16]), it does provide a handy policy *prescription* for a conservative-nationalist Republican president who might want to improve relations with Russia in order to reduce American involvement in NATO so that the United States can focus on China.

An America First administration could readily adapt an idea first floated by the president of France, Emmanuel Macron. In December 2022 Macron suggested that in any peace negotiations, Russia's fears that "NATO comes right up to its doors" should be dealt with by offering Russia security guarantees. The Biden administration immediately rejected this idea as a "non-starter," but a Republican president could go well beyond the scope of Macron's suggestion and instead embrace Russia's "legitimate security interests" to strike a grand strategic bargain with Russia regarding Europe and the countries of the former Soviet Union. In this bargain an America First president would recognize the "legitimate security interests" of the Russian Federation by ceding Moscow's dominance in the lands of "ancient Rus" as its legitimate sphere of influence; in return, Moscow would agree to end its war against Ukraine, although without returning any of the Ukrainian territory it had seized since 2014. In addition, in return for recognition of its sphere of influence, Russia would extend security guarantees to the existing European members of NATO and the European Union. Ukrainian objections to such a plan would be readily waved off by a Republican administration that had a negative view of the Zelenskyy government as corrupt.

Such a strategic bargain would allow an America First president to move on NATO as Trump had wanted to do in his first term. The Russian security guarantee to western Europe could be used as a justification for an American withdrawal from NATO. The only obstacle to such a move would be the correlation of forces in Congress. For while support for the alliance among elected Republicans in the House has been steadily declining, there is still considerable support for an active American contribution to NATO among Democrats and most Republicans in the Senate. The split between the MAGA and gentry Republicans has often been on display. The Senate resolution approving the admission of Finland and Sweden to NATO in August 2022 passed 95–1 with only two Trumpists deciding not to join the otherwise unanimous vote: Sen. Josh Hawley (R-Mo.) voted nay and Sen. Rand Paul (R-Ky.) voted "present."[17] Likewise, when DeSantis dismissed the invasion as a mere "territorial dispute," most of his critics were Senate Republicans. But this obstacle could be easily overcome. For it would not take a formal withdrawal, which would be unlikely to pass in the Senate, for the United States to neuter NATO. Instead, a conservative-nationalist president could readily implement what would be a de facto withdrawal from NATO — by ordering a drawdown, in other words, a progressive abandonment of a leadership role in the affairs of the alliance by American soldiers and diplomats at NATO headquarters in Brussels, a reduction in the U.S. armed forces based in Europe, and a slashing of financial support to the alliance.

Moreover, the America First logic for a reduction or elimination of the American leadership role in NATO would hold regardless of what happens in Ukraine. Even if the Russian Federation were defeated on the battlefield and forced to sue for peace, a conservative-nationalist president could still readily point to the elimination of the Russian threat to western Europe as a reason to leave the defence of Europe to the Europeans themselves.

Doubling Down on China

While Republicans might be divided on Russia, there is considerable agreement within the party on China and the challenge its rise poses to the United States. There are, however, substantial variations in those views. As president, Trump was fixated on the trade surplus that China enjoyed, and by all accounts was relatively unconcerned about the argument of some of his advisers and officials that China posed a geostrategic threat to American dominance in the Pacific Ocean — hardly surprising given Trump's more generalized indifference to America's global leadership. But that presidential indifference allowed the geostrategic hawks in the administration to ally with the protectionist America First enthusiasts concerned about trade to issue a National Security Strategy in December 2017 that officially identified both Russia and China as revisionist powers. "China and Russia want to shape a world antithetical to U.S. values and interests," it declared. "China seeks to displace the United States in the Indo-Pacific region, expand the reaches of its state-driven economic model, and reorder the region in its favor."[18]

Given this official characterization of China, it is not surprising that Trump's presidency was marked by a persistent hawkishness on China with the United States not only moving in June 2018 to impose harsh measures on a range of imports from China, but also to continue its attacks on Chinese tech firms such as Huawei Technologies Co. Ltd., of Shenzhen, intensifying what the *Los Angeles Times* has called America's "war against Huawei," a conflict that goes all the way back to 2003, when Cisco Systems of San Jose sued Huawei for stealing its operating system source code.[19] The declaration by the Trump administration that China posed a geostrategic threat to the United States not only reflected the views of the national security hawks in the administration, it also reflected a common view on the Democratic side of politics in the United States. Although the atmospherics of the Sino-American relationship improved somewhat after Trump was defeated, the Biden administration chose to keep many of Trump's China initiatives in place, such as the tariffs imposed against Chinese imports, sanctions in response to the crackdowns in Xinjiang and Hong Kong, measures to counter Chinese maritime claims in the South China Sea, and weapons sales to Taiwan. One measure of this bipartisan agreement is that when Kevin McCarthy, the new Speaker of the Republican-controlled House of Representatives, moved in January 2023 to create a committee with the unambiguously confrontational name "Select Committee on the Strategic Competition Between the United States and the Chinese Communist Party," 146 Democrats joined all 219 Republicans in approving it; just sixty-five Democrats voted against it.

Given the essential continuity in China policy between the Trump and Biden administrations, it is highly unlikely that a future conservative-nationalist Republican administration would change the American approach to China. If Trump himself returns to the White House, we are likely to see a resumption of the same essential hawkish incoherence in China policy that we saw between 2017 and 2021.[20] For Trump's views on China have not changed. He continues to try to arouse anti-China sentiment in the United States by calling COVID-19 "the China virus," claiming that China has "really destroyed the whole world" with COVID. He continues to claim (and perhaps he actually believes) that Chinese, not Americans, pay the costs of the tariffs that his administration imposed against Chinese imports. He continues to have an ambiguous view of General Secretary Xi Jinping. On the one hand, when an interviewer suggested that Xi was a "killer," Trump quickly agreed: "He *is* a killer."[21] On the other hand, given Trump's own authoritarian instincts, he cannot resist praising Xi for the "strength" that he seems to like so much in autocratic leaders. For example, at a campaign rally in Wilkes-Barre, Pennsylvania, in September

2022, he said admiringly that "he rules with an iron fist. 1.5 billion people. Yeah, I'd say he's smart."

But whether the next Republican president is Trump or another conservative nationalist, we are likely to see an intensification of conflict with China. For there is a logic of escalation at work in the relationship, particularly since China under Xi is in a comparably hawkish mood. The government in Beijing has adopted an increasingly assertive posture, eager to respond to every slight. It is inclined to interpret every Western move as an effort to contain China, or to stop its rise to great-power status, or to interfere in what Beijing asserts are properly its internal affairs. However, the escalatory dynamic has now reached the point where any move on either side to seriously dial down the hawkishness will be seized on by domestic opponents and criticized as inappropriate conciliation. This was certainly the result when Biden and Xi had a long, three-hour face-to-face meeting in Bali ahead of the G20 summit in November 2022. However, when the Ministry of Foreign Affairs of the People's Republic of China characterized the meeting as "candid and constructive," Biden was immediately hit with a wave of Republican criticism. Sen. Marco Rubio (R-Fla.) accused him of being "willing to sacrifice everything" instead of holding China "accountable for its rampant human rights abuses, ongoing theft of American intellectual property, and its refusal to investigate the origins of COVID-19." According to Sen. Tom Cotton (R-Ark.), Biden's "naive return to a policy of appeasement will hurt the United States, endanger Taiwan, and further embolden Xi Jinping." For her part, Sen. Marsha Blackburn (R-Tenn.) claimed that Xi's "sole interest is global domination, and he will readily take advantage of the Biden administration's weak foreign policy to inch closer to that goal." Given the intensity of such anti-China sentiments on the Republican side, an America First administration is likely to double down and harden its China response.

Because tariffs on Chinese goods are such a high-profile and obvious tool to "hit back" at China — and because it proved so easy for Trump to persuade gullible MAGA voters that it was the Chinese producers slapped with tariffs rather than American consumers who paid the added costs — an America First administration will be inclined to embrace tariffs as a tool of choice in its efforts to contain China.

But a Republican in the White House will also seek to intensify the effort to decouple the United States from China that had begun in a hesitant way under Trump, and was then continued and expanded by the Biden administration. After Biden took office, there was a constant barrage of executive actions against Chinese firms and organizations (or "entities"). In June 2021 Biden moved to expand a Trump-era executive order banning American investment in Chinese companies with ties to defence and surveillance sectors, identifying an additional fifty-nine firms. In December 2021 he signed the Uyghur Forced Labor Prevention Act, which imposes on importers the obligation of proving that forced labour in Xinjiang province was not used to produce goods. A variety of federal agencies were equally active. In 2021 and 2022, the U.S. Department of Commerce added eighty-seven Chinese firms and organizations to the Bureau of Industry and Security's "Entity List" and thirty-three entities to the "Unverified List," subjecting them to U.S. government licence requirements of various severity — by the end of the year, over 600 Chinese entities were on the lists. In March 2021 the U.S. Federal Communications Commission (FCC) added five Chinese firms to a blacklist that sought to steer investors and customers away from the firms. Later in the year the FCC terminated the right of a Chinese telecom to provide services in the United States. In December 2021 the U.S. Department of the Treasury blacklisted nine Chinese companies, banning Americans from buying and selling their shares. In May 2022 the U.S. Security and

Exchange Commission identified over eighty Chinese companies for possible expulsion from American exchanges. Other sanctions included a Department of Commerce ban on solar panel material from Xinjiang in June 2021 and export controls on semiconductors in October 2022. Given the steady drumbeat of measures targeting Chinese firms and other organizations under the Biden administration, it is highly unlikely that these efforts to target China will lessen under a Republican administration.

We can also expect that a Republican administration will not be able to resist following the America First playbook in the Pacific. Since Republicans have become as protectionist as Democrats used to be, a Republican administration is likely to continue to punish America's trading partners in the Indo-Pacific for "taking advantage of America." It will embrace the Trumpist tool of choice, tariffs, but it will also increasingly use other regulatory instruments in its security competition with China, and will continue to insist that America's trading partners follow its lead, as the case of Huawei Technologies demonstrates so well. It is likely to pursue a unilateralist path, steering well clear of multilateral institutions designed to boost free trade such as the Comprehensive and Progressive Agreement for Trans-Pacific Partnership (CPTPP) or plurilateral institutions such as the Digital Economy Partnership Agreement (DEPA). In the security realm, an America First president would likely reprise the approach to allies in the Pacific and would threaten to withhold security assistance from America's Asia-Pacific allies for "not paying their dues."

•

The kind of foreign policy that we might expect from a Republican conservative-nationalist president pursuing an America First agenda will likely be one that seeks to finish the job that Trump started between 2017 and 2021. The different elements of that agenda — limiting America's multilateral engagements, abandoning an internationalist leadership role for the United States in order to focus solely on the interests of Americans, trying to eliminate the imbalances in trade in goods with other countries — is likely to meld with a broader geostrategic agenda: resetting relations with the Russian Federation so that energy and focus can be concentrated on pushing back against China. But the abandonment of a leadership role in the maintenance of an American-led rules-based international order, when combined with a continuation of efforts by the People's Republic of China and the Russian Federation to undermine American leadership, will lead to a profound transformation of international politics as the American world is brought to an end.

5.

A POST-AMERICAN WORLD

If an America First administration moves to withdraw from an active geostrategic role in Europe while at the same time it ratchets up its response to China in the western Pacific, how will the other states of the West — all friends, allies, and trading partners of the United States — respond? Will they do what they did during Donald Trump's presidency between 2017 and 2021: sit tight, try to manage the America First approach to global politics as best as they can, and hope that American voters elect another "normal" president like Joe Biden? That is one possibility, if only because it worked between 2017 and 2021. However, the return of an America First Republican to the White House would clearly demonstrate to all of the other states of the West that the political system in the United States can no longer be trusted to dependably produce the same kind of government that it did between 1945 and 2016. In that event it may convince America's Western friends and allies that a new approach is needed. And that, in turn, may lead to the fragmentation of the West as a singular geostrategic entity.

The Fragmentation of the West

In Europe one likely consequence of the resumption of an America First foreign policy will be an intensification of discussions among members of the European Union over the development of European strategic autonomy — the idea that the EU should develop capabilities that would allow it to be autonomous from other powers and autonomous enough to conduct its own operations. In the past some Europeans did not conceive of strategic autonomy as a way to gain autonomy from the United States, but rather as a way to strengthen the transatlantic relationship. However, given that Trump actually declared in 2018 that the European Union was a "foe" of the United States,[1] it is likely that a resurgent America First administration will push Europeans into thinking about how to achieve a greater autonomy that is not necessarily linked to the United States.

Likewise, among the European members of the North Atlantic Treaty Organization, it is possible that the discussion that had begun when Trump was first elected will also intensify. As early as May 2017, after attending the NATO and G7 summits, Angela Merkel, the German chancellor, had openly worried about the future: "The times in which we could completely depend on others are, to a certain extent, over," she said. "I've experienced that in the last few days. We Europeans truly have to take our fate into our own hands." Two years later, it had become much clearer what America First under Trump actually meant for NATO: as Emmanuel Macron, the president of France, put it in November 2019, "To have an American ally turning its back on us so quickly on strategic issues; nobody would have believed this possible." Macron argued that "we need to draw conclusions from the consequences":

> The instability of our American partner and ris-
> ing tensions have meant that the idea of European

defence is gradually taking hold. It's the aggiornamento for a powerful and strategic Europe. I
would add that we will at some stage have to take
stock of NATO. To my mind, what we are cur-
rently experiencing is the brain death of NATO.
We have to be lucid.[2]

Now it is true that the Biden administration rescued NATO
from its slide into a comatose state. When Russia launched its full-
scale invasion of Ukraine in 2022, not only did Biden himself work
hard to rally the alliance to respond in a unified way, but members
of his cabinet, like Antony Blinken, the secretary of state, and Lloyd
Austin, the secretary of defense, and their department officials,
did the diplomatic legwork necessary to keep the alliance united.
However, if we see a resurgence of America First and an administration that seeks to dramatically reduce America's commitment to
its transatlantic partners, or to the broader international order that
was undergirded by that relationship, then NATO will surely be
more than brain-dead; it will be pining for the fjords.

It is possible that an America First administration might try to
resuscitate NATO by negotiating a "new" transatlantic alliance.
The idea of renewing the Atlantic alliance is not new: Philip H.
Gordon and Jeremy Shapiro, two former officials in the Democratic
administration of Barack Obama, envisaged what a "new" NATO
might look like. Writing nine months before Macron was declaring
NATO brain-dead, Gordon and Shapiro were certain that the alliance was in fact already completely dead, killed by Trump. Their
view was that the "old" NATO alliance was no longer viable given
changes in both global and domestic politics. They argued that
what was needed was an equal partnership: "The next alliance,"
they wrote, "cannot be only about channeling U.S. contributions
to European security; it must also be a global partnership to which

each side contributes in order to protect their mutual security and economic interests." This, they admitted, would require "both a U.S. president who recognizes its value and Europeans who are able to overcome their own internal divisions."[3]

However, given how America First Republicans view Europeans, it is unlikely that any Republican president that emerges from a nomination process dominated by MAGA Republicans would be inclined to see any value in an equal partnership with Europe. Because of that, it is likelier that the Europeans will be forced to restructure their defence arrangements in the face of an American withdrawal. Needless to say, there are huge obstacles in the path to European geostrategic integration. One obstacle is capacity. As presently structured, Europe simply does not have geostrategic strength without the United States. As the prime minister of Finland, Sanna Marin, frankly acknowledged in December 2022 in a speech during a visit to Australia: "I must be brutally honest with you, Europe isn't strong enough right now," she said. "We would be in trouble without the United States." But it is possible that a Republican administration will finally push the Europeans into serious political and geostrategic integration as the best way to "take our fate into our own hands," as Merkel advocated in 2017.

Another obstacle is the ambiguous geostrategic position of the United Kingdom, which is a member of NATO but no longer a member of the EU. In the event of a transatlantic unravelling triggered by a new administration in Washington and the emergence of a more integrated European approach to defence, several geostrategic options would be open to the U.K. (assuming, of course, that the kingdom continues to remain united, and is not undone by the Scottish, Welsh, and Irish nationalisms that roil British politics). One option would be to remain outside the European Union but contribute to, and participate in, the development of an integrated European defence policy. Or the government in

London, Conservative or Labour, could use the American withdrawal from Europe as an opportunity to undo the huge damage that Brexit did to the British economy, and seek to rejoin the EU (and hope that the EU takes them back). Or it could turn into a kind of latter-day Orwellian Airstrip One, increasingly disconnected from Europe geostrategically, clinging instead to whatever would remain of the historical "special relationship" under an America First administration.

While the obstacles are significant, the countries of Europe have the potential for considerable strength globally if they were pushed into further geostrategic integration by American policies. Without the United Kingdom, Europe has a population of more 450 million and a GDP of $16.6 trillion. With the U.K., a more integrated Europe would have a population of more than 523 million; its GDP would be $19.9 trillion, roughly equal to that of the United States. While Europe has a significant geostrategic weakness in its energy and raw materials dependence on others, together, the Europeans have capacities in many of the areas that would be necessary to achieve strategic autonomy. Needless to say, actually achieving that "togetherness" would be exceedingly difficult. Efforts to achieve strategic resilience, much less strategic unity, continue to founder on the rocks of national preferences. However, European geostrategic autonomy, while difficult, is not impossible. The same logic of integration that resulted in the formation of the United States of America in the 1770s, the Dominion of Canada in the 1860s, or the Commonwealth of Australia in the 1890s could well operate in Europe in the 2020s and 2030s. And skeptics might be reminded that geopolitical surprises can often concentrate the mind and produce very sudden turns.

In the Pacific, by contrast, we are likely to see a different dynamic play out if an America First president comes to office, and resumes treating the countries of the West in that region as Trump did between 2017 and 2021. While the America First view is that the alliance in Europe is a drag on the United States, perhaps even obsolete, as Trump used to claim, in the Pacific, where an America First administration is likely to ramp up confrontation with China, the United States very much needs friends and allies. And it is not at all clear that a conservative-nationalist administration will be able to manage the very friends and allies it needs to compete with China.

As it is, the four countries of the West in the western Pacific — Japan, Korea, Australia, and Aotearoa New Zealand — have all been engaged in a balancing act for the last five years, trying to navigate between an increasingly assertive China and an increasingly combative America.[4] For all of them share a common dilemma: they all depend on China economically and the United States geo-strategically — in other words, they have relied on American dominance in the western Pacific for their security. And none of them wants to have to choose between the two great powers contesting for dominance in the Pacific.

But what Hugh White of Australian National University has called "the China choice" is in fact being forced on all of these countries by how the United States has decided to respond to China's rise. In a prescient essay written in 2010, White predicted that a rising China would eventually choose to challenge, rather than just accept, American hegemony in the Pacific. He suggested that the United States had three choices: it could resist China and try to preserve its hegemony in the region; it could withdraw and let China establish dominance in the western Pacific; or it could share power with China by forging a "concert system" in the Pacific similar to the Concert of Europe of the nineteenth century, when the great powers worked with each other to maintain the settlement put in place by the Congress of Vienna of 1814–15 that ended the Napoleonic War. White predicted that while some Americans might prefer to "walk away" and leave the countries of the western Pacific to sort things out for themselves, most Americans would choose the first option. (He argued that while the concert option would represent the best outcome for everyone, he thought that Americans would never accept any option that required the United States to be just one among equals.)[5]

The decision of the United States to stay and contest the Chinese challenge — eventually formalized in the Trump administration's National Security Strategy of 2017, and reconfirmed by the Biden administration's Indo-Pacific Strategy of 2022[6] — poses a number of challenges for American friends and allies in the western Pacific. First, it will require that all countries of the West in the region make that very choice that they have tried so assiduously to avoid. For while the Biden administration has been at pains to stress that in a free and open Indo-Pacific, "governments can make their own choices,"[7] in effect friends and allies of the United States will not be given much leeway by Washington in how they choose to deal with China. If they choose not to comply voluntarily with American export or other regulatory controls employed against China, Washington will, as Evan A. Feigenbaum, a former senior State Department official, so bluntly but correctly put it, "bring the hammer down" and coerce compliance. In Feigenbaum's view the present zeitgeist in Washington thus creates a "collision" with whatever foreign government is not onside with the United States.[8] All Western governments felt that pressure during the Biden administration — an administration that actually cared about American allies and American leadership. The hammer will be significantly less pleasant under an America First administration that openly denigrates America's allies.

The second challenge is that it is not clear how these four countries would react if an America First administration started pursuing a seriously bellicose policy toward China that sought to accelerate decoupling or pushed China militarily. All of them have generally supported the American presence in the Pacific for the security and stability it has brought. But would any of them actually give full-throated support for an American policy that increased the likelihood of a slide into a more robust confrontation? For in each of these countries, we have seen a similar pattern: China's assertive policies under Xi Jinping have hardened both public attitudes and government policies. But it is not clear that there is unwavering support for whatever policies Washington chooses to pursue against China.

Under Kishida Fumio, the Japanese government has hardened its position toward China. At the 2022 Shangri-La Dialogue summit, Kishida promised to increase Japanese defence spending as part of his government's "realism diplomacy for a new era." Without mentioning China by name, he drew an explicit comparison with Ukraine. "I myself have a strong sense of urgency that 'Ukraine today may be East Asia tomorrow,'" he said. "We must be prepared for the emergence of an entity that tramples on the peace and security of other countries by force or threat without honoring the rules."[9] This generally reflects Japanese public opinion, which has a favourable view of the United States and the American military presence in the region and on bases in Japan. Moreover, a significant percentage of Japanese surveyed in 2021 — 82 percent — agreed that if they were forced to choose, they would choose to strengthen relations with the United States even if that would sour relations with China. But if given a choice, half of those surveyed would prefer to maintain strong relations with the United States and develop relations with China.[10] This preference reflects the general approach to the great-power confrontation between China and the United States in the last decade, and suggests that Hatoyama Yukio, a former Japanese prime minister, was correct when he suggested that there would be little support in Japan for being dragged into a war over Taiwan, for example.[11]

In the Republic of Korea, there was already considerable ambivalence about Washington's containment strategy during the Biden administration. It is true that Yoon Suk Yeol, the conservative People Power Party candidate, won the March 2022 presidential election campaigning on a platform of a "deeper alliance" with the United States, a "retooled" relationship with China, and "closer" relations with Japan.[12] But Yoon's victory over his rival from the Democratic Party of Korea, which has a much more cautious view of great-power competition in the region, was exceedingly narrow — just 0.73 percent. Moreover, the Democratic Party has a commanding majority in the National Assembly. American efforts to push South Korea into becoming more antagonistic toward China would surely expose those divisions.[13]

In New Zealand, as in other Western states, there has been a significant and rapid hardening of public sentiment against China, and an increase in how warmly New Zealanders feel toward the United States (a shift that maps to the election of Joe Biden).[14] But while the government in Wellington has been increasingly moving in solidarity with other Western states on broad geostrategic issues, there is little indication that either of the major parties — the centre-left NZ Labour Party or the centre-right National Party of New Zealand, would respond positively if an America First president amped up the pressure on Wellington to take a more confrontational approach to China.[15]

Even in Australia, where the alliance with the United States is so revered that the government endows the word with a capital A, we are unlikely to see a willingness to simply follow the United States unthinkingly in a drift to war.[16] It is true that the Australian government has been an enthusiastic participant in the robust American response to the rise of China, beginning with Obama's "pivot to Asia" in 2012 that saw U.S. Marines stationed in Darwin; Australia was the first of the Five Eyes intelligence alliance to ban

Huawei, which it did in 2018; and Canberra took the initiative that led to the creation of an Australia–United Kingdom–United States security partnership, known as AUKUS, in 2021. Under Scott Morrison's Coalition government, there was even a willingness to frame defence policy in overtly warlike terms. The prime minister himself warned Australians that the geopolitical situation was more serious than at any time since the 1930s — a not-so-coded reminder to Australians of how the country had been threatened by an invasion by Japan in 1942, and how it had been subsequently "rescued" by the Americans. Morrison's minister for defence, Peter Dutton, was less coded, speaking openly of preparing for war with China. "The only way you can preserve the peace," Dutton said on ANZAC Day in 2022, "is to prepare for war, and be strong as a country. Not to cower, not to be on bended knee and be weak. That's the reality."[17] The election of an Australian Labor Party (ALP) government in May 2022 shifted the rhetoric, but not the substance. Prime Minister Anthony Albanese was explicit that "strategic competition in the region informs our view of our relationships with nations in the region." To that end he launched a defence review, and has promised to "spend whatever was necessary to produce the defence force that could defend Australia." In March 2023 the Albanese government announced a $368 billion deal to acquire a fleet of nuclear-powered submarines by the 2050s. Between three and five Virginia-class submarines would be acquired from the United States in the 2030s; a new class, the SSN-AUKUS, would be developed with the United Kingdom using American nuclear technology; the five Australian SSN-AUKUS submarines would be built in Adelaide and delivered in the 2040s and 2050s.[18]

However, while both the rhetoric and the substance of policy has prompted Hugh White to worry that Australia was on a "sleepwalk to war,"[19] it is possible that when actually confronted with the likelihood of a drift into armed conflict, a different definition of the national interest will emerge and lead Australians to choose an alternative option. Peter Varghese, the former head of an Australian intelligence agency, the Office of National Assessments, may be more widely reflective of Australian opinion. In a widely quoted essay, Varghese argued that it was not "an abandonment of the alliance to assert that the maintenance of U.S. primacy, however desirable, is not a vital Australian interest."[20] Public opinion polls reflected his view: they suggest that Australians have their "eyes wide open" not only on the possibility of war, but also on whether it would be in Australia's interests to follow the United States into a conflict with China. While fully 87 percent of Australians believe that the alliance is important for Australian security, 77 percent of the same respondents agreed with the statement that "Australia's alliance with the U.S. makes it more likely that Australia will be drawn into a war in Asia that would not be in Australia's interest."[21] The work of political scientists Peter K. Lee and Andrew Carr on how Australia's three prime ministers before Albanese — Tony Abbott, Malcolm Turnbull, and Scott Morrison — responded to great-power competition in the Pacific shows that each of these leaders defined the Australian national interest in distinct ways, suggesting that "the path Australia ultimately chooses to follow is perhaps less predetermined than structural explanations might have us believe."[22] Emma Shortis, a historian at RMIT University in Melbourne who focuses on American politics, goes further: in her exploration of the implications for Australia of a return of a Trumpist in the White House, Shortis argues that it is possible that Australians could rethink and reimagine the "capital-A Alliance" in the years ahead and seek to transition it from an alliance premised on the inevitability of war to one focused on threat reduction.[23]

In short, even a cursory look at the domestic politics in each of these four states of the West suggests that it is unlikely that an America First administration in Washington would find fertile soil in any of them for the kind of approach that it would likely pursue. The America First playbook, after all, calls for a completely transactional approach to friends and allies: hector them to comply with Washington's demands, and if necessary, coerce them — on the assumption that they will bend because they have no other alternative than dependence on the United States. Thus we could expect an America First administration to push ahead with efforts to decouple from China, oblivious of the economic harms this causes to its allies. We could expect Washington to impose protectionist tariffs in retaliation for "ripping off Americans," but closing off American markets to goods and services, and reshoring supply chains for good measure. And all of this will be accompanied by a chorus of whingeing about what free riders America's so-called friends and allies are.

If a Republican administration actually tried to do this, however, it is likely that the relationships with the other countries of the West in the western Pacific would be seriously and permanently damaged. But these four states — alienated by an America First administration — would not have the option that Europeans — discarded by that administration — have. In Europe there are several factors that could aid in a pivot to real strategic autonomy: a wide range of existing interstate institutions, deep economic and political integration, geographic proximity, and sheer numbers of states of different sizes and capacities. In the Pacific the four Western states have none of these advantages.

First, there might be a complex architecture of regional international institutions, but none is organized around the four Western states themselves. All four are members of larger regional organizations like the East Asia Summit and the Asia-Pacific Economic Cooperation forum. All four are also signatories to the various trade agreements that have proliferated in the Pacific over the last decade: the Comprehensive and Progressive Trans-Pacific Partnership, originally proposed and then abandoned by the United States; the Regional Comprehensive Economic Partnership, which grew out of a joint Chinese-Japanese initiative in 2011. They are also members of the Indo-Pacific Economic Framework for Prosperity, an initiative launched by the Biden administration in 2022 to foster economic cooperation between the United States and thirteen countries in the western Pacific. Australia, New Zealand, and Japan are members of another Biden initiative, the Partners in the Blue Pacific, a partnership that also includes the United Kingdom, designed to boost cooperation in economic and diplomatic linkages with Pacific Island countries. Australia and New Zealand are members of the Pacific Islands Forum with Japan and South Korea recognized as dialogue partners. The institutions with a geostrategic focus include the military alliances with the United States, which involve hub-and-spoke arrangements: bilateral collective defence treaties for Japan and Korea, and a trilateral security treaty with Australia and New Zealand (ANZUS, though the United States suspended its defence obligations to New Zealanders in the 1980s, so that today New Zealand is not considered an ally, but a "close strategic partner"). Only Australia is involved in AUKUS, the security partnership with the United Kingdom and the United States. The Quad involves two of the allies, Japan and Australia, though Korea and New Zealand are members of a grouping known as the "Quad Plus." The Five Eyes intelligence alliance includes Australia and New Zealand, though Japan and Korea collaborate in "Five Eyes Plus" arrangements.

The lack of an institutional structure where the four Western states could seek collective comfort is compounded by patterns of trade. The top trading partner for each of them is China. Approximately 22 percent of all Japanese trade is with China; for South Korea, 27 percent; for Australia, 26 percent; and for New Zealand, 28 percent. The United States is the second most important trading partner for

Japan (19 percent) and Korea (15 percent), third for New Zealand (11 percent), and fourth for Australia (9 percent). Trade among the four states themselves trails far behind: the other three countries are in the top five trading partners for Australia and New Zealand, Australia and Korea are in Japan's top five, but only Japan is in Korea's top five partners.[24]

Finally, while it has become fashionable to argue that geography no longer matters in an era of globalization and instantaneous communication, the physical distances that separate the countries of the West in the western Pacific are significant: Korea and Japan are separated from Australia and New Zealand by 8,000–10,000 kilometres. What Australians refer to as the "tyranny of distance"[25] means that there are none of the opportunities for closer integration of the sort that one can find in Europe. It is thus possible that Japan, South Korea, Australia, and Aotearoa New Zealand might find themselves seriously at odds with the United States as a result of an administration with an America First playbook, and decide to push back hard against American efforts to push them into open confrontation with China.

But there is another possibility, one raised originally by White in his 2010 essay. All of America's allies in the western Pacific have to worry that, while the United States might initially step up to try to resist the Chinese challenge to its hegemony, Americans will quickly discover that the costs of doing so will increase dramatically. These costs will inevitably prompt Americans to ask themselves if it really is in their interests to remain engaged. So it may well be that a Republican president would ramp up the strategic competition with China, alienating America's allies and partners in the western Pacific in the process. But then it might look at the significant costs to Americans that standing up to China involves, and decide that it is not worth the candle, and withdraw, in effect leaving China as the dominant power in the western Pacific.[26]

Either way, then, whether by alienation or by abandonment, the four states of the West in the western Pacific would find themselves alone. In such circumstances they would likely make their peace with the new regional hegemon and seek an accommodation. They would likely do so both on a bilateral basis with Beijing, and multilaterally through the many other international institutions in the western Pacific — since all non-Western countries would also find themselves needing to readjust to the new regional order.[27]

A New Era in Global Politics

The possible futures sketched out above are, needless to say, highly speculative. But they flow logically from the observation that the America First form of conservative nationalism in United States foreign policy seems to be fundamentally incompatible with the kind of internationalist and multilateralist approach to the world that was pursued by every American administration, Republican and Democrat, from the 1940s to 2017, and from 2021 to 2025. By contrast, America First celebrates isolationism and unilateralism. It denigrates the idea that international politics involves a "society of states" that work together to develop rules to make the anarchy of international politics more predictable and manageable.[28] As two of Trump's senior advisers put it, the administration they worked for had "a clear-eyed outlook that the world is not a 'global community' but an arena where nations, nongovernmental actors and businesses engage and compete for advantage. We bring to this forum unmatched military, political, economic, cultural and moral strength. Rather than deny this elemental nature of international affairs, we embrace it."[29] Certainly, America First celebrates a distinctly anachronistic mercantilist view of international trade that denies the benefits of comparative advantage and routinely ignores trade in services. It cheers the dislike of the Other — a logical extension of the deep embrace of nativism, racism, and xenophobia domestically. We saw all these attributes on display between 2017 and 2021, and it would be logical to see a return to those dynamics should Trump, or another America First Republican, become president. And just as the essential unity of the geostrategic West depended on an America that was internationalist, multilateralist, liberal, and democratic, we can readily see how — and why — an America First president, backed by a Republican Party that is both deeply anti-democratic and illiberal, but eagerly supported by tens of millions of Americans, could readily break that unity.

Could the fragmentation of the West sketched out here — the Europeans pushed into creating greater strategic autonomy and the states of the West in the western Pacific pushed into making their peace with China — set in motion a feedback loop within the American political system? It is possible that American corporations with bottom lines that will be negatively affected by the end of Western unity might rethink their financial support for the GOP. It is possible that, if the foreign policy disruptions of a second America First administration were profound enough, large numbers of American voters would come to recognize, even if only belatedly, that the American-led rules-based order was worth keeping. This might, in turn, lead either to a purge of the GOP's anti-democratic, illiberal, authoritarian, and racist elements, or even to the emergence of a new party. In short, it is possible that both of America's parties will once again be dominated by leaders and elected members of Congress who have internationalist beliefs.

However, from the perspective of 2023, the prospects of a feedback loop working in this fashion seem dim. Parties do not purge themselves. The Republican Party would have to be pushed, and there is only one exogenous push that would work: corporations, wealthy donors, and small-dollar contributors would have to stop donating money to the GOP; voters would have to stop voting for Republican candidates at the federal, state, and local levels — from president all the way down to the proverbial municipal dogcatcher. Judging by the 2022 midterms, however, there is no evidence that this is likely to happen any time soon: the vast sums of money flowing into Republican coffers from corporations, megadonors, and small-dollar donors alike, and the hundreds of millions of votes that were cast for thousands of Republican candidates up and down ballots across the United States, demonstrate that huge numbers of Americans are deeply okay with the Republican Party just as it is. It might be added that Republicans no doubt take considerable comfort knowing that voter suppression and voter apathy persistently protect them against electoral punishment. In 2022, 130 million of the 240 million Americans who were eligible to vote did not make it to the polls, some because they were victims of successful voter suppression, almost exclusively in Republican-controlled states, but most because they simply couldn't be bothered to show up.

Even if such a feedback loop in the United States were to bring an internationalist-minded president to the White House in the next decade, it might be too late to stop the collapse of the American world. The bonds that link other states of the West to the United States have only so much elasticity. The Trump presidency from 2017 to 2021 stretched those bonds; another America First presidency would likely break them. Moreover, other Western states are unlikely to be willing to organize themselves geostrategically on the basis of unpredictable quadrennial swings in the pendulum of American politics. Thus, it is likely that another America First administration would herald the end of the American world as we have known it since the 1940s, and mark the beginning of a new era in global politics.

In the discipline of International Relations, giving names to particular eras bracketed by key dates is such a common conceptual device that we often take their names and dates for granted.[30] In the last century, we have had three distinct eras: the interwar era (1919–1939) was followed by the Cold War era (1945–1991). This, in turn, was followed by the post–Cold War era, commonly dated as starting in 1991 with the end of the Soviet Union. Until 2022, however, there was little agreement on when this era ended. Some argued that the attacks of September 11, 2001, marked an appropriate end date; others suggested that the global financial crisis of 2008 marked the end; and still others argued for ending the era with the COVID-19 pandemic that began in 2020. That debate came to an end with the Russian Federation's full-scale invasion of Ukraine. There is now common agreement with the timely proclamation by Emma Ashford of the Scowcroft Center in a *New York Times* op-ed on February 24, 2022, the very day that the invasion started: "It's official: The post–Cold War era is over."[31]

So far, however, there is still no name for the new era. And if Americans continue to elect presidents like Joe Biden who value American leadership in global politics, then we really do not need a new name, and can just wait until one bubbles up and is widely accepted. In the meantime we could follow the lead of Roland Paris of the University of Ottawa: his tongue firmly in his cheek, Paris called it what it technically is: the "post-post-Cold War era."[32] But if a Republican who is committed to pursue a MAGA America First agenda comes to power, then it would be useful to have a name not simply to distinguish the new era from the post–Cold War era (1991–2022), but also to distinguish it from the much longer period of American leadership in global politics.

One way to distinguish that long stretch of American global dominance — a dominance that for friends and allies of the United States in particular made their world an *American world* for so many years — would be to appropriate a name suggested by political commentator Fareed Zakaria. In 2008 Zakaria published a bestselling extended essay entitled *The Post-American World*.[33] Published just months before the global financial crisis reached its destructive peak in September 2008, the book was an exploration of broad shifts in global power that had occurred in the early twenty-first century. Zakaria argued that the very success of the United States in establishing and maintaining an international order that encouraged massive increases in global trade and globalization had led to a significant shift in power. Unlike other analysts writing at the time who saw the United States as a "declining" power in global politics,[34] Zakaria insisted his book was not about American decline, but rather the "rise" of everyone else in global politics. His "post-American world" was one in which the United States was still the dominant power with "a stronger hand than anyone else — the most complete portfolio of economic, political, military, and cultural power,"[35] but one in which there were many more centres of power and a greater complexity in global politics. Most important-ly, in Zakaria's post-American world, the United States was still an engaged, multilateral player, still keen to play an active, and con-structive, leadership role in world affairs; indeed, political scientist Christopher Layne has opined that Zakaria should have entitled his book *The Now and Forever American World*, because the book argued that the United States was not about to be replaced as a leading power any time soon.[36]

By contrast, the post-American era envisaged here will differ markedly from Zakaria's. The United States will still have that "stronger hand" globally. Americans will still devote more of their wealth to defence than all the other major powers combined, and as a result the United States will still have the superordinate military capacity that it enjoyed during the post–Cold War era, particularly the ability to project military power on a global scale. It will still have huge economic power, a function of its diverse, technologic-ally advanced, innovative, and productive economy. The U.S. dollar will still be the world's dominant reserve currency (even if that dominance is likely to come under increasing pressure if global confidence in the United States dims as a consequence of American domestic dysfunctions). American culture will continue to entertain the world. American universities will continue to be an intellectual magnet. And the United States will remain the world's most sought-after destination for immigration.

But in the post-American era, the United States will be in a very different geostrategic location. Its imperial footprint will be considerably diminished as the global system of friends and allies built up over eight decades gets slowly (or rapidly) torn down by ham-fisted America First policies and the purposive cession of global leadership to others. Americans will no longer be the dominant rule-setters in global governance, as that function will pass to other states, and as other powers find ways to work around what is likely to become American unilateralism and obstructionism. In short, in the post-America era, the United States will become an ordinary power — still a great power, but an *ordinary* great power, no different than the other great powers that will struggle with each other for dominance in the years ahead.

The transition to the post-American era will have profound consequences for all friends and allies of the United States as they try navigate the new world in which America might still be a dominant power but no longer the leader of the West.[37] But no one will be more affected by the arrival of the post-American era than Canadians.

6.

NAVIGATING A NEW WORLD

In 2003, as the United States was at what turned out to be the apogee of its unipolar moment, Lloyd Axworthy, the foreign minister in the Liberal government of Jean Chrétien between 1996 and 2000, published an idealistic book outlining a Canadian foreign policy for what he called a "new world." It was a vision for an independent Canadian foreign policy that rejected American hegemony and unilateralism. It sought an alternative to "a world dominated by military force and naked self-interest."[1] *Navigating a New World* was a comprehensive and carefully argued policy brief for a program of policy advocacy for remaking a very different world than the one that he had to deal with as foreign minister.

Axworthy was worried about American unipolar dominance and how to navigate around it. Twenty years on, American unipolarity is not only well in the past, but the geostrategic environment has also shifted so dramatically that by 2020 there was in the West a widespread nostalgia for a return of American global leadership — a nostalgia that the presidency of Joe Biden was able to satisfy.

But, with apologies to Axworthy, I have argued in this book that there still may be an entirely new world to navigate if politics in the United States unfold in a particular way in the next several years. If an America First Republican returns to the White House, we may be looking at precisely the kind of post-hegemonic America that Axworthy was wishing for in 2003. And in that event, Canadians, like all others in the West, will have to navigate a world in which the United States, under the banner of America First, will purposely abandon the global leadership that every president except Donald J. Trump embraced during the Cold War and post–Cold War eras, and instead forge a unilateral path in global politics, as Axworthy himself put it so aptly in 1996, "without regard to the legitimate interests of others."

Living in a Post-American World

What would the arrival of the kind of post-American world sketched out in this book mean for Canadians? How would Canadians be affected if the United States were no longer willing to play the leadership role that it once played? What would happen if the American-led rules-based international order were replaced by the kinds of worlds imagined by Vladimir Putin, Xi Jinping, or Donald J. Trump? For, as political scientist Roland Paris reminds us, the way these leaders conceptualize sovereign statehood differs markedly from how sovereign states are treated in the American world.[2] What would life be like for Canadians in Putin's world, where countries not able to defend themselves are not considered "real" sovereign states, but just "colonies" to be conquered, dominated, or eliminated at will by the more powerful? Or in Xi's world, where a rejuvenated China is at the centre, with smaller states knowing their proper place? Or in Trump's world, which is simply an arena where nations compete for advantage, with its implication that to the stronger competitors always go the spoils? How would Canadians be affected by a fracturing of the West that would likely be triggered by the return of an America First conservative nationalist with the Europeans growing more unified and getting into more quarrels with a protectionist America, and the countries of the West in the western Pacific seeking their own accommodations with a China that will refuse to be contained by the United States?

These geostrategic shifts will not occur all at once nor immediately after a Republican conservative nationalist is in the White House; therefore, the impacts of the end of the American world, at least as they are felt by Canadians, will emerge over time. Effects in two broad areas can be identified, however.

CANADIAN-AMERICAN RELATIONS

The United States that Canadians will have to deal with if a Republican America First president returns to the White House will ironically look somewhat like the United States in the early twentieth century. In that era Americans might have called their country a liberal democracy, but anti-democratic practices and illiberalism pervaded American life and politics. Black Americans, Native Americans, and women were systematically denied the vote. In huge swaths of turn-of-the-century America, the liberal ideal of equality only applied to those who were male and White. Violence against Black Americans, including lynchings and racial "cleansing" of neighbourhoods, was common; such violence was visited on Black Americans by both the state and their fellow White citizens. Discrimination based on skin colour was widespread and legitimized in law, reflecting the power of the individual states. It was not until the middle of the twentieth century that changes in ideas about rights prompted a slow growth of both liberal and democratic practices, including the use of federal power to limit the rights of states to impose illiberal local laws on their citizens.

But in the years ahead, Canadians will have to deal with a polity in which tens of millions of American citizens have abandoned the ideals of liberal democracy for a form of government and politics that defies easy characterization. Over the last decade, the U.S. Supreme Court has rolled back federal authority, returning more power to the states. The conservative supermajority put in place as a result of Republican manipulation during the Trump administration will ensure that in future, the United States will not be so united: there will be "free" and "unfree" parts of the country as red and blue states choose their own liberal and illiberal paths.[3] Moreover, the Republican Party has become the political home for a popular movement that is clearly anti-democratic, illiberal, authoritarian, and anti-constitutional. That movement glorifies political violence and wishes for a strongman leader. It is built on resentment and the desire to return to an imagined glorious past. It is also deeply racist.

Given these characteristics, some see this turn in American politics as fascism or a variant thereof: proto-fascism, neo-fascism, or, as President Joe Biden characterized it in August 2022, "semi-fascism."[4] Some, playing on a favourite Chinese Communist phrase, have called it fascism with American characteristics.[5] Others, however, are more hesitant. They worry, as the writer George Orwell did in 1944, that the f-word gets used so "wildly" that it becomes "almost entirely meaningless"; instead, Orwell suggested, we should "use the word with a certain amount of circumspection and not, as is usually done, degrade it to the level of a swearword."[6] For others, preserving the meaning of the word is key. Tom Nichols of *The Atlantic*, for example, argues that what we see today is "pre-fascist" rather than fully fascist. Rather than the disciplined militias of the European fascist movements of the 1920s and 1930s, the MAGA movement today is dominated by too many out-of-shape, well-off, and bored suburban Americans narcissistically cosplaying at being revolutionaries. And Trump himself, according to Nichols, was "too incompetent, too lazy and selfish, to lead an actual fascist movement." But, he argues, Trump paved the way for a real fascist movement "by corroding the guard-rails of the American system, normalizing the kind of rhetoric and attacks on opponents used by actual fascists, and convincing or-dinary American voters that mass violence is an alternative to the ballot box."[7] In other words, we need to reserve the f-word for when real fascist leaders and a real fascist movement appear in the United States.

But whatever term we use to describe the contemporary turn in American politics, the results — the attempts to suppress the votes of Black Americans; the attempts to skew electoral outcomes through widespread partisan gerrymandering; and the efforts of Republicans and their supporters on the Supreme Court to turn the clock back on civil rights, women's reproductive rights, and LGBTQ+ rights — gives today's America a distinctly *fin de siècle* vibe.

Among the consequences of these shifts in American politics that Canadians will have to deal with in the future is the likelihood that we will see a further increase in cross-border movement of Trumpism's populist, illiberal, authoritarian, and White nationalist ideas. Copycat adoption of American political rhetoric and ideas by Canadians is nothing new in the relationship: Canadian anti-war protestors during the wars in Vietnam and Iraq used the same slogans as their American counterparts. We saw the same phenom-enon during the COVID-19 pandemic, when anti-government, anti-authority, anti-masking rhetoric and ideas migrated northward across the border. But the "Trump effect" has also galvanized more extreme right-wing populism in Canada, as Barbara Perry, the dir-ector of the Centre on Hate, Bias and Extremism at the Ontario Institute of Technology, and her colleagues have documented.[8]

The phenomenon was clearly on display during the "Freedom Convoy" trucker protest that occupied and disrupted downtown Ottawa for a month in 2022. Symbols, slogans, ideas, even the flags — the upside-down national flag, some "Trump 2024" flags, the Confederate battle flag, the Gadsden flag (including a Canadianized version with a Canada goose instead of a timber rattlesnake and the words DON'T TREAD ON ME, EH) — were copied from American protests. References to First Amendment rights, or the slogan "2022 is 1776," reflected the degree to which protestors were Americanized if not American (since there were some Americans among the convoy protestors). The protest also had a transnational element. A number of Americans were involved in the organization of the protest, and Americans also donated to the convoy's GoFundMe account. American political, corporate, and media figures — Donald Trump, Elon Musk, and Sean Hannity and Tucker Carlson of Fox News — weighed in to offer their support; Trump ally Mike Lindell, CEO of MyPillow, even tried to ship pillows and bibles to the truckers (though he and his truck driver were turned back at the border because they were not fully vaccinated against COVID-19).

Reflecting the cross-border movement of Trumpist ideas, in 2023, the Eurasia Group's annual "Top Risks" assessment featured Canada for the first time, suggesting that Canada was "showing signs of contagion" from the United States. Political parties were becoming more polarized, policy issues were being weaponized, and exposure to the American social-media ecosystem was radicalizing Canadians.[9] In short, it is likely that Canadians will have to deal with the "Trump effect" in the years ahead.

The Canadian response to this contagion in the future will likely be an intensification of the negative response to Trumpist politics that we saw in the aftermath of the trucker convoy. Already we have seen the willingness of Canadians to voice their opposition to political developments in the United States. For example, Women's Marches in the United States had their counterparts in Canada (and in many other Western countries, often held outside U.S. embassies and consulates). After the murder of George Floyd, a Black civilian, by a White police officer in Minneapolis in May 2020, protests were held in fifty-nine Canadian cities and towns, in all ten provinces and three territories. We may see an increase in anti-American sentiment in response to the growth of illiberalism in the United States — similar to the surges in anti-Americanism in the late 1960s during the administration of Richard Nixon, or in the 1980s during Ronald Reagan's presidency, or in the early 2000s in response to George W. Bush. And if that happens, it will complicate the relationship, for anti-American sentiment in Canada always affects how disputes between the two countries are resolved.

Most Canadians take how disputes with Americans are resolved for granted, a reflection of the complexity and the pervasive reach of the Canadian-American relationship. Occasionally, however, the relationship does bubble to the surface — when there is a dispute between the two governments, or when a U.S. government policy triggers protests in Canada, or when an American president visits Canada, and there is an opportunity to engage in what John W. Holmes, a former Canadian diplomat, has called "the blandishments of hands-across-the-border oratory."[10] But most Canadians simply do not reflect on just how unusual the Canadian-American relationship is in international relations. Rarely does one find a great power — indeed, in this case, a hyperpower — that persistently chooses to treat its smaller and much weaker neighbour with forbearance. Over the last century and a half, the Canadian-American relationship has been marked by a willingness of the United States to use its great power judiciously, and usually with an eye to ensuring that its northern neighbour remained essentially friendly. This is not to suggest that when Canada and the United States get into a quarrel, power is completely absent; rather, the United States has been willing to take Canadian interests into account in the outcomes of those disputes. Nor is it to suggest that American interests have not always been served by such outcomes. Rather, it is to suggest, without being Pollyanna-ish, that a diplomatic culture of conflict management emerged over the course of the twentieth century. As K.J. Holsti of the University of British Columbia put it more than fifty years ago, Canadian and American officials shared a common view that conflicts of interest between the two countries were "'problems' to be solved" rather than "confrontations to be won at all costs."[11]

The free trade agreements that the United States has entered into with Canada — the sectoral agreements in defence production in the 1950s, in autos and auto parts in the 1960s, the comprehensive Canada–United States free trade agreement of 1988, and the North American Free Trade Agreement that came into force in 1994 — were all predicated on the persistent willingness of a succession of American governments, Democratic and Republican, to ensure that the interests of Canadians were served despite the massive power differential between the two countries. Moreover, this approach synced well with the general approach of American administrations in Washington to allies and friends around the world — a willingness to play the long game rather than seeing relationships in purely transactional terms where power can be applied against the weaker to ensure an unbroken string of zero-sum wins.

However, once the United States was no longer in the business of global leadership, it no longer would need to play the kind of long game that it has played with its friends and allies for the last eighty years. This, combined with the heightened protectionism inherent in the America First agenda, would affect Canadians. It would mean that trade disputes — the commonest cause of conflicts between the two governments — would proliferate. Importantly, however, an America First administration would no longer be inclined to treat either of its North American trading partners as though the rules mattered: both Canada and Mexico would likely discover that lodging protests about American protectionist practices using the dispute settlement mechanism of Chapter 31 of the USMCA/T-MEC/CUSMA/ACEUM would be increasingly difficult. And using the World Trade Organization would no longer be an option, since it is likely that a Republican administration would continue the policy, begun under Trump, of blocking appointments to the Appellate Body, a policy continued by the Biden administration. It is likely that trade rules will atrophy further in the absence of American leadership.

Other difficulties in the relationship would result from the increasing polarization in American politics. In particular, dealing with elected Republicans at both the federal and state levels will be exceptionally more difficult than with elected Democrats, particularly with those Republicans who have bought into their leader's characterization of the Canadian prime minister as a "far left lunatic" or Canada as a country of "left-wing fascists."[12] Likewise, diplomacy with elected Republicans in Congress or with governments in red states in a "post-truth" era will complicate matters further. Republicans at both the federal and state levels have been so willing to promote, Nazi-style, *die große Lüge* — the Big Lie — that they have normalized lying about public matters, including policy issues. When wild conspiracy theorizing and "alternative facts" (the term that Kellyanne Conway, one of Trump's counsellors, used in an attempt to justify his administration's easily disproved lies) are accepted as "truth," it is not clear that the kind of fact-based exchanges that always marked Canadian-American policy-making in the past will even be possible.

Finally, much of the Canadian-American governmental relationship occurs at the bureaucratic level, part of what political scientists call "transgovernmental relations."[13] The relationship is deeply institutionalized and bureaucratized with cross-border patterns of bureaucratic interaction between officials in federal and state agencies. In a number of policy areas, organizations have been created to manage the relationship. In defence, a binational command, the North American Aerospace Defense Command (NORAD) was created in the 1950s, deeply embedding Canadians in a continentalized scheme for the protection of North America. Boundary waters are regulated by a binational commission, the International Joint Commission (IJC), created by the Boundary Waters Treaty of 1909. Canadians have the same number of seats as Americans in making decisions that are binding on citizens on both sides of the border.[14] At the provincial and state levels, there is a similar institutionalization with cross-border organizations covering a number of areas, including energy, fire-fighting, management of the electricity grid, and managing highways and bridges. However, as political scientist Wilfrid Greaves has reminded us, the organizational cultures of many of the agencies that deal with Canadian-American relations, such as Homeland Security, Defense, Customs and Border Protection, and the Office of the U.S. Trade Representative, have been influenced by Trumpism, which may have implications well into the future.[15]

In short, the Canadian-American relationship in a post-American era will inexorably reflect what is happening more broadly in international politics. An America First administration, seeking "confrontations to be won at all costs" in an environment that is marked by great-power domination in their own spheres of influence and few global rules, will be unlikely to behave toward Canada as internationalist administrations did during the Cold War and post–Cold War eras.

CANADA'S GLOBAL ENGAGEMENT

If the post-America era is marked by the kind of fragmentation of the West sketched out in the previous chapter, the "new world" that Canadians will have to navigate in the years ahead may, paradoxically, look somewhat like an "old world" that Canadians once lived in — the international system of the first part of the twentieth century.

Two similarities between these worlds stand out. First, the new world of the 2020s and 2030s, like the old world before 1939, will have more than the one great power of the unipolar post–Cold War era. But exactly how many is a matter of debate among scholars of International Relations. Some argue that we are returning to bipolar configuration of the Cold War era with the United States and China as the two poles of power in a so-called G2 world. Some have suggested that the system will be tripolar, since the Russian Federation, with its nuclear weapons, must be seen as a great power. Others still see the emergence of a multipolar system with many great powers. In addition to the orthodox range of poles (unipolar, bipolar, tripolar, and multipolar), we can find other imaginative descriptors, such as interpolarity or uni-interpolarity. Even a world *without* poles has been envisaged: a-polarity, non-polarity, or a "G-zero" world.[16]

Readers might be forgiven for thinking that academics wondering about how many great powers there will be sounds a little like medieval inquiries into how many angels can dance on the head of a pin. But, as Benjamin Zala of Australian National University argues, we need to recognize that polarity is an important facet of contemporary global politics, primarily because great powers and others act on their perceptions of how many poles of power there are.[17]

If an America First president comes to power, and the West fractures in the way sketched out in the previous chapter, it is possible that the post-American world will turn out to be quadripolar. In International Relations, this is an unusual category, for normally scholars use only four categories of polarity: unipolar, bipolar, tripolar, and multipolar. Daron Acemoğlu, an economist at the

Massachusetts Institute of Technology, makes the case for a quadripolar system. He argues that a bipolar system dominated by the
United States and China would not be able to deal effectively with
global issues like artificial intelligence, human rights promotion,
and climate change. He proposes creating a quadripolar system by
adding two further poles of power to the mix: the European Union
and what he called a "consortium of emerging economies" that included countries like Brazil, India, Indonesia, Malaysia, Mexico,
Türkiye, and South Africa.[18]

Acemoğlu's quadripolar system is explicitly *normative* — in his
view, these *should be* the four poles of power necessary to deal more
effectively with global problems. By contrast, the quadripolarity I
envisage emerging in the 2020s and 2030s is *empirical* — in other
words, these *will be* the four great powers in the years ahead. In
this view the two dominant powers will be the United States and
China. A third great power would be a more united and more deeply integrated Europe, capable of acting as a united geostrategic actor
in global affairs, even if not yet a singular, sovereign, and federat-
ed United States of Europe. The Russian Federation, weaker and
poorer, but nonetheless nuclear-armed, would be a distinctly fourth
power. While not as multipolar as the system during the first part
of the twentieth century — when the great powers included the
United Kingdom, France, Germany, Italy, Japan, the Soviet Union,
and the United States — the quadripolar system that Canadians
would likely have to deal with in the future would echo the pre-
1939 world.

The second similarity is that the new post-American world, like
the old world of the early twentieth century, will be a world in
which there is no longer any American global leadership — except
perhaps in the minds of those nostalgic for the past. In the early
twentieth century, the United States might have been a great power,
but it was an ordinary great power. Before 1939 Americans might

have entertained notions about their exceptionalism in the world, but they demonstrated little leadership, particularly after the abandonment of the League of Nations in 1919. It was not until the Second War broke out in September 1939 that Franklin Delano Roosevelt began to exercise the kind of clear leadership that would vault the United States into a position where that sense of American exceptionalism became synonymous with global leadership and the conceit of hegemonic stability theory, in which a selfless hegemon provided security and stability for the good of the world as a whole. The abandonment of that global leadership role — what Stephen Saideman of Carleton University has jokingly dubbed "hegemonic abdication theory"[19] — and a return to being an ordinary great power as the United States was in the early twentieth century will be a key feature of the new world.

However, there is one way in which the new world that Canadians will have to navigate in the 2020s and 2030s will be quite unlike that old world of the early 1900s. In the early twentieth century, Canadians were all alone with their American neighbours in North America. But that solitude was eased by the fact that their political community, the Dominion of Canada, was not the independent and sovereign state that it was to become in December 1931, but still part of an empire that stretched around the globe. It is true that those who lived in Canada then did not have identical geostrategic sentiments toward the Empire of which they were a part. English-speaking Canadians, so many of whom had bonds of family with the "mother country," had a broader geostrategic connection of kinship beyond North America that made contributing to the wars of the Empire not only natural, but imperative. French-speaking Canadians, by contrast, had been completely cut off from their "mother" since the Conquest in the 1760s, so that by 1900 what connections there were to France were more symbolic than familial. Because their ties to the Empire were legal rather than emotional, most French-speaking Canadians tended to have little interest in contributing Canadian blood or treasure to fighting the Empire's wars — as we saw in the case of the Boer War and the First World War. Indigenous peoples in Canada had a special, and separate, relationship to the Imperial Crown, through the Royal Proclamation of 1763; but by the early 1900s, the practices of settler colonialism in Canada had erased whatever discrete geostrategic connections might have evolved — an erasure that, as Hayden King of the Yellowhead Institute eloquently argues, continues today.[20]

In the new world of the 2020s and 2030s, by contrast, it is likely that there will be fewer of the multilateral connections that during the Cold War and post–Cold War eras had provided Canada with the benefits of having a seat at the table and being able to draw on the support of like-minded friends in advancing Canadian interests — and offering some relief for Canada's geostrategic solitude in North America.[21] Instead, it may be, as the historian John English surmised in 2012, well before the geopolitical shifts surveyed in this book were fully apparent, that Canada, the United States, and many other nations will be prompted "to retreat to their own fastnesses and turn away from the wobbly international institutions created in the twentieth century."[22] Without other countries of the West to provide multilateral connections across the Atlantic and Pacific Oceans, or in the circumpolar north, Canada will indeed be all alone with the Americans. Canadians got a limited preview of this during the dispute with Saudi Arabia in 2018. When Canada's foreign minister, Chrystia Freeland, called for the release of human rights activists in Saudi Arabia, the government in Riyadh responded by expelling the Canadian ambassador, withdrawing Saudi students from Canadian universities, and suspending commercial negotiations. As political scientist Roland Paris notes, not a single Canadian friend or ally, anywhere in the world, backed Canada.[23] If the post-American era brings the geostrategic realignments bruited in this book, that loneliness will likely be a more common experience as the multilateral global landscape changes. For with fewer tables to have a seat at, and fewer clubs with like-minded friends, Canada's global role will diminish.

In a post-American world, we will see a slow transformation in the Canadian government's geostrategic links across all three of its oceans. During the Cold War and post–Cold War eras, Canada's geostrategic links to Europe were always strong with Canada a relatively active contributor to NATO's European operations. But those links were forged in a fundamentally *North Atlantic* context — in other words, involving both the United States and Europe. If America's North Atlantic link frays, Canada's links with Europe will fray too. This will be particularly marked if a conservative-nationalist president makes good on Trump's promise to withdraw from NATO. And if Europe undergoes a strategic re-orientation as a result of the return of an America First president, there will be little room for Canada as a *European* partner, particularly if a geostrategic rivalry emerges between a more united Europe and the United States.

A similar shift is likely to emerge in the Pacific. In the fall of 2022, the government of Justin Trudeau reshaped Canada's foreign policy posture when it released its Indo-Pacific Strategy, billed as a response to a "once-in-a-generation global shift that requires a generational Canadian response." The government outlined a plan to deepen Canadian involvement in the Pacific over the next decade in five areas: peace and security; trade, investment, and supply-chain resilience; people-to-people initiatives; sustainability and a green future; and initiatives to increase Canadian presence in the region. The government committed $2.3 billion in funding over the next five years to what it termed a "whole-of-society" strategy.[24] The shifts in Canadian foreign policy in 2022 recognized, even if only belatedly, all the compelling arguments for increasing

Canada's role in the Pacific.[25] But in order to be taken seriously as a fully engaged Indo-Pacific actor, the government now faces two problems. First, it must overcome the drag of what I have called the "North Atlantic anchor" — that tendency to give priority to our overseas engagement in Europe.[26] Second, it will have to find a way to overcome the lack of public support in Canada for "geostrategic spending" — in other words, spending on the full range of whole-of-government activities in geostrategic affairs: foreign affairs, defence, intelligence, cyber, trade, immigration, public diplomacy, and development assistance. Moreover, the new focus on the Pacific may come too late. If Canada's geostrategic links across the Pacific are relatively shallow and underdeveloped during a presidency that takes America's allies seriously, those links will thin considerably if the countries of the West in the western Pacific are pushed by an America First president into an accommodation with China.

The same dynamic will be at work in the circumpolar north. The present structures and institutions for multilateral engagement in the Arctic are already under stress because one of the members of the Arctic Council, the Russian Federation, held the chairmanship from 2021 to 2023, and the other members decided to "pause" all the meetings of the Council and its subsidiary bodies as long as Russia was at war against Ukraine. If the United States under an America First administration decided to withdraw from the Arctic Council in order to pursue a more robust unilateral policy in the Arctic, the circumpolar region would become much more politicized than it already is,[27] with the United States, Russia, and China all contesting Arctic waters, and the multilateral forums like the Arctic Council or the Inuit Circumpolar Council might be sidelined.

In short, if the American world that Canadians have lived with since the 1940s is transformed into a post-American world, the government's general approach to foreign policy posture will not really fit that new world. Canadian foreign policy remains designed for a world in which the geostrategic West is a relatively united singularity of some fifty independent states, and the United States is an active and engaged leader of the West, willing to use its superordinate power and capabilities to help forge and maintain a global order for the anarchical society that is world politics. If that world is transformed, Canadians will need to rethink their foreign policy.

What impact will this shift in Canada's global engagement have? Because Canadians have been so used to not having to take international politics seriously for so long — the case for this has been made most succinctly and persuasively by political scientist Thomas Juneau[28] — most are unlikely to even notice their government's shrinking engagement if we drift into a post-American era. Some Canadians may be affected by shifts in the global capitalist system that will occur as decoupling intensifies, and policies designed to create supply-chain resilience alter the location of value chains — and the higher costs to the consumer that will be inexorably associated with them. Others may be affected by the greater protectionism that will come with an America First administration and an increasing willingness to hit Canadian goods and services with protectionist measures. Others still who have family and other links to countries around the world will be affected by the profound shifts that geopolitics will bring in political alignments — as those Canadians with ties to China, Hong Kong, and Taiwan are already experiencing as relations between China and the West have spiralled into frostiness, distrust, and hostility.

By contrast, all Canadians will be affected by one change that is likely to occur if the geostrategic changes outlined here come to pass: a radical shift in defence spending. The more than $23 billion that the Canadian government spends on defence each year is for armed forces that were — and remain — designed for an American world. Canadian forces are structured to be able to contribute to that enduring trinity of missions: to be "strong at home, secure in North America, and engaged in the world," to use the words of the 2017 defence white paper.

But those defence missions will change if there is no longer a set of geostrategic partners "in the world" to be engaged with, and it is likely that the government in Ottawa will be pushed by a conservative-nationalist administration in Washington into re-shaping the Canadian Armed Forces to contribute more directly to an America First geostrategic agenda. At minimum this could involve spending more robustly on military capacity in the Arctic to satisfy American concerns about the security of their northern flank. It could include expanding a boots-on-the-ground military presence in the Arctic, and expanding year-round polar icebreaking capability by acquiring additional naval icebreaking capability to complement the CCGS *John G. Diefenbaker*, the Canadian Coast Guard's heavy Polar Class 2 icebreaker that will come into service in 2029, and the Royal Canadian Navy's much lighter Polar Class 5 Arctic offshore patrol ships (AOPS), acquired by the Conservative government of Stephen Harper in 2007. At maximum it might involve an American expectation that Canadian defence spending would be geared to assist American efforts in the western Pacific to contain China. We could also anticipate that an America First administration would come to office with a highly negative view of Canadian "easy riding" on defence, discussed in Chapter 1. Even if a Republican administration does not have the kind of protection-racket view of allied defence that Trump had, it is unlikely to be happy with the raw numbers: Americans spend 3.3 percent of GDP on defence; Canadians spent just 1.4 percent. An America First administration will not likely be the kind of tolerant ally that Canadians have been used to in the past.[29]

Canadians will also be affected by the transformation of the international order in other, more indirect, ways. The shift of an

America First administration away from multilateralism and toward a more robust unilateralism will have a profound effect on global governance. Issues that are global in scope and impact, like climate change and extreme weather events, ocean pollution, food security and famine, or the management of pandemics, cannot be dealt with unilaterally. It is possible that other great powers will step in to keep global governance alive: for example, a more united Europe could work with China, India, and other like-minded smaller powers on global issues. But the success of global governance depends on the involvement of *all* great powers. If the United States is absent, or, worse, becomes obstreperous and obstructionist, effective global governance is in serious doubt. One need only look at the 1930s to see what can readily happen when great powers like the United States remain aloof from international politics.

The engagement of great powers is particularly important for the maintenance of global peace. The kind of geostrategic shifts that have been bruited in this book do not usually produce day-to-day effects that are immediately evident — until, that is, all of a sudden they are. The profound transformation of Canadians' lives in the middle of the summer of 1914 and over the Labour Day weekend in 1939 is a reminder not only of the fragility of systemic peace, but also of the speed with which it can collapse. The threat of systemic war is a constant feature of global politics, since great powers always have the ability to plunge the world into a general conflict.

The intensity of that threat will vary, however. After the Russian invasion of Ukraine, commentators on Russian state media started threatening the use of nuclear weapons, talking points echoed on right-wing media in the United States. In January 2023 the Bulletin of the Atomic Scientists moved their Doomsday Clock — a meta-phorical clock that since 1947 has sought to warn the public about the threat of the destruction of the world through technology — to

90 seconds to midnight. Likewise, the steadily increasing tensions between China and the United States continue to prompt references to "Thucydides's trap." In 2012 Graham T. Allison, a political scientist at Harvard University, coined the term to explain why China and the United States were "destined for war" (as he entitled his 2017 book).[30] The "trap" is derived from the succinct explanation offered by the Athenian historian Thucydides for the long and ruinous war between Athens and its Delian League allies and Sparta and the Peloponnesian League in the ancient Greek world: "What made war inevitable was the growth of Athenian power and the fear which this caused in Sparta."[31] The "trap" appeared to describe the trajectory of Chinese-American relations; Allison's thesis was even discussed by Barack Obama and Xi Jinping at a summit in 2015.[32]

Despite the increasing tensions between the great powers, the likelihood of a general systemic war is relatively low. This is partly because the logic of nuclear deterrence that prevailed throughout the Cold War continues to operate today, and partly because of the size and power of the West. Like those in other Western countries, Canadians benefitted over the eight decades after the end of the Second World War from the existence of a relatively united geostrategic bloc of Western states led by the United States. But that could readily change if the unity of the geostrategic West is fractured by an America First administration. A world in which that Western bloc has fragmented and American leadership has evanesced is a world in which systemic peace will be less assured.

What Can Be Done?

How could Canada prepare for the possibility that a conservative nationalist will return to the White House? Suggestions about how to "Trump-proof" Canadian foreign policy initially focused on the possibility that Trump would secure re-election in 2020; since then, the focus has been on the possibility of a resurgence of the America First agenda under a Republican president.

THE TRANSOCEANIC PRESCRIPTION

A common thread in much of the commentary about how Canadians should deal with a possible return of America First fixes on the importance of developing and strengthening relations with other states in the international system; finding like-minded states to work with; and seeking strength in numbers in order to challenge America First initiatives. Roland Paris, director of the Graduate School of Public and International Affairs at the University of Ottawa, has argued that the currents of global politics, particularly the global assault on liberal democracy, "should be a wake-up call for Canadians." He suggested that to meet the challenges of the contemporary global environment, Canadians needed to rethink their historical approach to international politics. "Canada will need friends and partners to provide the safety of numbers. Establishing closer working relationship with like-minded democratic states should be a top priority."[33]

Expanding and deepening friendships around the world was also the recommendation of the late Greg Donaghy, a historian and director of the Bill Graham Centre at the University of Toronto, and Thomas Axworthy, public policy chair at Massey College. Donaghy and Axworthy suggested "rebuilding" relations with the countries of the Arctic Council, and with Mexico and other states in Latin America; "relaunching" Canada's presence in Africa; and strengthening ties with Japan, whom they characterized as "almost as alone as we are."[34] It was a view echoed by Kerry Buck, a former Canadian ambassador to NATO, who argued that one of the solutions to what she called the "new world of strategic surprise" was to widen friends and partners across different regions of the world, and find ways to use ideas and diplomacy to make a distinct space for Canada in the new architecture that will be created, just as Canadians did after the Second World War.[35]

Richard Albert, a professor of law, and Allan Rock, a former minister in the Liberal government of Jean Chrétien and a former ambassador to the United Nations, suggested that Canada should engage in diplomacy with key allies to create a "co-ordinated and mutually reinforcing strategy" to ensure the protection of multilateral commitments to environmental protection, disarmament, and international financial institutions. They also recommended that Canada should lead the creation of a new forum for the world's democracies, extending Biden's Summit of Democracies and transforming it into a more permanent means of coordinating a collective response among America's friends and allies to what they characterized as "the coming attack on democracy" that would occur if Trump returned to power.[36]

Scott Gilmore of *Maclean's* magazine even recommended that, in anticipation of "another Trump," Canadians should abandon what he characterized as the badly leaking American ship of state and instead "build a new foreign policy alignment in anticipation of the next American wreck." He recommended that if the United States no longer shared Canada's foreign policy goals — a rules-based international system, support for human rights, and strong Western institutions like NATO, for example — Canada should think about applying to join the European Union.[37]

For some analysts, the key lies in diversification not only of partners, but also of trade. Thus, for example, among the five "moves" that Irvin Studin of *Global Brief* magazine suggested Canada should make to counter America First in the long run is the diversification not only of Canada's global partners, but also of its huge trade dependence on the United States, which Studin recommended be driven down to 40 percent of Canadian trade by

2030.[38] Political scientists Robert W. Murray and Tom Keating also focus on expanding Canada's links with other countries, though they argue that Canada should not just concentrate on like-minded democracies. Rather, they argue for the importance of reaching out to a range of different countries, using multilateral fora like the G20 to tackle global issues.[39]

Given how important transoceanic links — across the Atlantic, across the Pacific, across the circumpolar north, and globally in its links to the Commonwealth, Organisation internationale de la Francophonie, and a huge range of international organizations — were to Canadian foreign policy during the Cold War and post–Cold War eras, it is perhaps not surprising that so many analysts would channel Christopher Walken and recommend that the only prescription for the America First fever is more transoceanic engagement.[40] Certainly, the idea of diversifying Canada's overseas links and Canadian trade as a way to reduce dependence on the United States is not new. The Liberal government of Pierre Elliott Trudeau embraced the same strategy in the 1970s with the "Third Option," which sought to strengthen Canada's ties with Japan and Europe.[41] Diversification is also an eminently sensible proposal in theory: as Irvin Studin noted, this is what serious countries do to survive.

But strengthening Canadian links to a range of countries beyond North America, whether like-minded democracies or key regional actors, would not solve Canada's geostrategic problem. In the contests and rivalries that will develop between the United States and other great powers in the 2020s and 2030s, Canada would find itself stuck as little more than a geostrategic appendage of the United States — possibly the only one if an America First administration successfully manages to alienate its allies in Europe and the western Pacific.

THE CONTINENTAL PRESCRIPTION

In 2001, as the Canadian government was considering how to manage its relations with the United States in the months after the terrorist attacks of September 11, political scientist Denis Stairs suggested to a parliamentary committee that they should keep just one priority in mind: "Maintaining an effective relationship with the United States," he said, "is the only true imperative in Canadian foreign policy."[42] That advice tends to guide the second set of prescriptions: should an America First administration return to power, focus on working with, and around, that administration. If one's goal is the maximization of Canadian well-being, then truly nothing else matters.

Most suggestions begin by encouraging whoever is prime minister to look back at the relatively successful playbook adopted by the government of Justin Trudeau when Trump took office in 2017. Trudeau adopted a broadly strategic approach to Canada–United States relations that — whether he realized it or not — had Stairs's advice at its core. The strategy included tight message control, careful personnel selection, and the range of assets deployed to press Canadian interests.

Although in opposition Trudeau had had a tendency to make off-the-cuff gaffes,[43] as prime minister his statements about Trump were always highly disciplined, taking the form of a mantra from which he never deviated. Whenever he was asked his opinion of some Trump outrage, Trudeau always gave a variant of his response to a question at a news conference in Calgary in January 2017 about whether he thought that Trump was a misogynist. "It is not the job of a Canadian prime minister to opine on the American electoral process," Trudeau responded. "It is the job of the Canadian prime minister to have a constructive working relationship with the president of the United States and that is exactly what I intend to do."[44] He also imposed the same tight message discipline on his caucus.

Trudeau also recognized the importance of personality and expertise. Even before Trump's inauguration, Trudeau shuffled his cabinet, transferring Chrystia Freeland from the international trade portfolio to foreign affairs. Freeland not only had a good grasp of the trade portfolio that promised to be front and centre in Canadian-American relations under Trump, but she also had a considerable network of contacts in the United States from her time as a journalist and editor in New York City.

Finally, the Trudeau government deployed as many diplomatic and political assets as possible to press Canadian interests in the United States. In what was known in Ottawa as an "all-hands-on-deck" approach to the relationship, Trudeau brought policy-makers with knowledge and experience, such as former prime minister Brian Mulroney, into the policy process. Canada's diplomatic and political assets were deployed widely across the American political system, embracing not only Congress, but state and municipal governments in what one observer called a "doughnut strategy" — in other words, working around the "hole" that was the Trump White House. Trudeau even reached out to Ivanka Trump, the president's daughter, in what was described as "daughter diplomacy" (prompting John Higginbotham, who had been the minister in the Canadian embassy in Washington from 1994 to 2000, to observe, "It is just so *Game of Thrones*").[45]

It is true that this strategic response only worked for a while. Trump was simply too seized by resentment and anger at American allies, and too hypersensitive to anyone who criticized him. Just as he eventually turned on other Western leaders who tried hard to keep him happy, such as French president Emmanuel Macron and Japanese prime minister Abe Shinzō,[46] so, too, did he eventually turn on Trudeau. In June 2018, after Trump had left the G7 summit in La Malbaie, Québec, Trudeau was asked about American tariffs that had been imposed on Canada by the Trump administration on the grounds that Canada was a national security threat. Trudeau gave the answer that he had given many times before: that he found the measures insulting. From Air Force One, Trump immediately tweeted that Trudeau had lied at his press conference and was "very dishonest & weak." Trump's advisers piled on: Peter Navarro, his trade adviser, told Fox News that "there's a special place in hell for any foreign leader that engages in bad faith diplomacy with President Donald J. Trump and then tries to stab him in the back." On CNN Trump's economic adviser Larry Kudlow accused Trudeau of "betraying" Trump, warning that "POTUS [President of the United States] is not going to let a Canadian prime minister push him around." In September 2018 Trump also turned on Chrystia Freeland, who was at the time Canada's lead in the free trade renegotiations. He told supporters at a fundraiser that she "hated America," and called her "a nasty woman," his favourite phrase for women he dislikes.[47]

But while the Trudeau government's "all-hands-on-deck" strategy did not immunize his government from Trump's idiosyncrasies, it does provide a durable model for the future. As Richard Albert and Allan Rock noted in their suggestions on how to protect Canada should Trump be returned, the first priority had to be to "buttress our trade access to the United States" by lobbying elected representatives of states with substantial trade with Canada: representatives and senators in Congress, state governors, members of state legislatures, and mayors. That strategy had worked well when the Trump administration targeted the North American Free Trade Agreement.

It also provides a guide for particular steps that the Canadian government could take right now to prepare for the possibility of a return of an America First agenda in Canadian-American relations. Thanks to an initiative that the Canadian embassy in Washington has run for the last thirty years, Canadian diplomats know precisely how much trade each congressional district, and each American state, does with Canada, and provide employment numbers and dollar values to that data. The effectiveness of this data tool suggests that the federal government could readily expand its lobbying operations in the United States. At present, Canada has consulates-general in thirteen American cities, spread strategically around the United States: Atlanta, Boston, Chicago, Dallas, Denver, Detroit, Honolulu, Los Angeles, Miami, Minneapolis, New York, San Francisco, and Seattle, and other offices in Houston, Palo Alto, and San Diego. But the very success of these missions in making the Canadian case to Americans at a local level suggests that Canada's official footprint in the United States could be even further expanded to state capitals and major municipalities. It also suggests that the federal government could assist provincial governments in expanding their missions in the United States.

Expanding Canadian diplomacy and greater engagement of American legislators are strategies that are also endorsed by Stuart MacKay, a Canadian historian of the Republican Party in the United States. But to help "Trump-proof" Canada, he goes further and offers concrete policy recommendations that he suggests should be embraced right now, during the Biden administration. To finesse, and blunt, Republican obsession with two issues — border security and allies "taking advantage" of the United States in defence — he suggests that Canada should step up its spending in two policy areas. First, Canada should forge an independent and well-funded strategy for assisting development and reducing poverty and insecurity in the countries of the Northern Triangle — El Salvador, Guatemala, and Honduras — that are the source of so many migrants seeking to move to the United States to escape poverty and violence. MacKay argued that if Canada launched a major development assistance effort in the Northern Triangle, it would demonstrate to Republicans that Canadians were trying to do something about an issue of overweening concern to them. Second, he suggested that Canada should radically ramp up its defence spending as a way of blunting persistent Republican attacks on America's alliance system.[48]

STARTING A CONVERSATION: A PROPOSAL

To prepare for the possibility that an America First administration may return to power, the Canadian government needs to begin the process of starting a conversation with Canadians about their changing geostrategic environment.

One way to initiate that discussion would be to adopt, but adapt, an idea proposed in 2021 by Thomas Homer-Dixon, a political scientist who works on threats to global security. Concerned about the state of democracy in the United States, and the dangers that the assault on democracy could have on Canada, he suggested an institutional solution: a non-partisan parliamentary committee with MPs from all parties. All members would be given security clearances so that they could be briefed on confidential matters relating to Canada–United States relations, and would be charged with providing specific guidance to the government on "the dangers we face and a clear vision of how to get past those dangers to a good future."[49] If such a committee were to be given a broader remit to cover the full range of the Canada–United States relationship, it would provide a means to explore not only the dangers that Canada is likely to face in the future, but also a means to bring Canadians more fully into the conversation about their most important international relationship.

But Canadians also need to start reflecting on the wider global geostrategic environment as well. To be sure, in 2022 the Trudeau government began to make tentative shifts in Canadian foreign policy in response to changes in global politics. In a series of ministerial speeches, a number of new initiatives were announced that served to bring Canada closer in line with United States foreign policy, particularly in the Indo-Pacific. Over the course of the fall, four ministers — Chrystia Freeland, the deputy prime minister; François-Philippe Champagne, minister of innovation, science, and industry; Mélanie Joly, minister of foreign affairs; and Anita Anand, minister of national defence — all gave speeches announcing policy shifts in their portfolios.[50] But what was missing in the ministerial line-up was the prime minister himself. Trudeau chose not to take an opportunity to explain to Canadians why his government was shifting direction. Likewise, his government made little effort to provide an overall framework so that Canadians could see the broader picture of the evolution of their country's foreign policy in the contemporary geostrategic environment and be given an opportunity to discuss policy alternatives.

It has now been two decades since the government in Ottawa provided Canadians with an opportunity to have a discussion about their geostrategic future. In 2002 Bill Graham, then the minister of foreign affairs in the Liberal government of Jean Chrétien, launched a foreign policy dialogue on what Canada's foreign policy priorities should be "in the face of new global realities."[51] That dialogue was a successor to an initiative launched early in Chrétien's ministry: the National Forum on Canada's International Relations was designed to provide public input into the foreign policy process. While these efforts had limited reach, and were heavily managed by officials, they at least provided some opportunity to involve Canadians about foreign policy priorities and what lay behind them. No government since then has bothered to try to involve Canadians in a dialogue about their country's engagement in global affairs. The Liberal government of Paul Martin (2004–2006), the Conservative government of Stephen Harper (2006–2015), and the Liberal government of Justin Trudeau since 2015 all simply *made* foreign policy without any effort to involve the public.

Nor did the Harper or Trudeau governments even bother to try to explain foreign policy to Canadians through the usual process of a foreign policy review. This process of review normally results in a formal government statement, usually a white paper. The last foreign policy review in Canada was undertaken in 2005 by Martin. Neither of his successors saw any necessity of reviewing foreign policy.

Given the profound shifts in global politics since 2005, it is surely past time for the Canadian government to initiate a review. But a number of observers think that this should not be an ordinary review of the sort that the Liberal government of Pierre Elliott Trudeau initiated in the late 1960s, or the Progressive Conservative government of Brian Mulroney held in the mid-1980s, or the reviews conducted by the Chrétien and Martin governments. The reviews conducted by Trudeau *père* and Martin were dominated by the bureaucracy with limited public and parliamentary input. By contrast, the Mulroney and Chrétien reviews were conducted by special parliamentary committees with considerable public input.

Instead, the model that is proposed for this review is the Royal Commission on the Economic Union and Development Prospects for Canada — the commission appointed by Trudeau *père* in 1982 and headed by a former minister of finance in his government, Donald S. Macdonald. The Macdonald Commission was well financed, independent of the government of the day, and undertook detailed studies on a range of topics. Its final report was not issued until after Pierre Trudeau had been replaced by Brian Mulroney. The three-volume report, running to over 2,000 pages and backed up by a vast library of seventy-two volumes of academic research specially commissioned for the project, recommended that Canada embrace comprehensive free trade with the United States, a recommendation that was accepted by the new Mulroney government.

The Royal Commission model for a foreign policy review, advocated first by Roland Paris of the University of Ottawa in October

2019, and echoed the next year by Jean-Christophe Boucher of the University of Calgary,[52] has a number of benefits. The prime benefit would be that the process of examining future foreign policy options for Canada would be out of the hands of both elected members of Parliament in Cabinet and the civil servants in Global Affairs Canada and the Department of National Defence. As Boucher put it bluntly, one would not want to leave the review to a government whose thinking about Canadian foreign policy "is worn-out, overly content to hold on to our past glory, or to obsess about being a world leader in something ... anything."

A Royal Commission would also have the kind of freedom to discuss matters openly that governments simply do not have. No Cabinet minister is in a position to discuss sensitive issues such as the likely impact that American politics will have on Canada frankly and freely without having to worry that a clip of the comments will go viral in the MAGA media ecosystem in the United States. The ability to talk freely — and thus possibly undiplomatically — about the tectonics of contemporary global politics is crucial for providing Canadians with a better understanding of the political challenges — and the mounting tax bills that will invariably come with taking geostrategic challenges more seriously — that they will face in the years ahead.

CONCLUSION

"The United States of America is greater than any administration," the Canadian diplomat-turned-scholar John W. Holmes wrote in *Life With Uncle*, his essay on the Canadian-American relationship, "and its progress has always been cyclical. Many administrations have scared us, but we have found new terms of agreement. Dr. Jekyll usually triumphs."[1] *Life With Uncle* was written in 1981, just as the Republican administration of Ronald Reagan was taking office. To some Canadians at the time, the Reagan administration did look like a scary Edward Hyde. The "new Right" was in the ascendency. The Conservative Political Action Committee saw four of the six liberal senators on its 1980 "hit list" go down to defeat. The Moral Majority had a catalogue of books to ban and television programs to supress. Reagan's domestic political agenda promised a right-wing tilt. In foreign policy Reagan had campaigned on the slogan "Let's make America great again" and came to office determined to assert American power in foreign policy. There were fears about how the conservative Reagan administration would treat Canada: "The Reagan era has begun, for better or worse," a Canadian journalist wrote after the inauguration. "There has been some trepidation expressed in the press that, so far as Canada is concerned, it will be for worse."[2]

Holmes's reminder provides an appropriate epigraph for this speculation on the future of Canadian foreign policy. In this book I have sought to sketch out, in an admittedly speculative way, a longer-term future scenario of likely possibilities for Canada should the American-led rules-based international order drift into disuse or collapse altogether. That order is already being pushed and challenged by the governments in Beijing and Moscow, which is why this book looked at the origins and evolution of the assertiveness of the People's Republic of China under its paramount leader, Xi Jinping, and the revanchism of the Russian Federation under President Vladimir Putin. It is the significance of those challenges to the American world that makes the "assault from within" launched by Trump in 2017 so important. For the American-led world order cannot survive unless the president of the United States, backed by Congress, and, ultimately, the citizens (and taxpayers) of the United States, is willing and able to lead.

I take seriously the possibility that Donald J. Trump could return to the White House in January 2025. Writing in the spring of 2023, I recognize that the tea leaves and other auguries available to the *chatterati* are at best unclear. There are those who are convinced that Trump is done; there are those who are equally convinced that ruling Trump out is the kind of magical thinking that convinced so many in 2016 that Americans couldn't possibly elect him president. Today, a number of elected Republicans are not at all keen to keep their political fortunes hitched to the Trump Train, but few appear to be willing to distance themselves from the former president and his MAGA supporters. According to McKay Coppins of *The Atlantic*, Republicans he talked to "repeatedly" expressed the hope that — how to put it genteelly? — "the situation will resolve itself naturally: He's old, after all."[3]

But politics is always about more than one individual, and the shifts we have seen in American politics will most assuredly out-live Trump. And so, if not Trump, the Republican candidate in 2024 will likely be a candidate beholden to the Republican Party's MAGA base. Moreover, there are various paths to the White House for a Trumpist Republican, including the possibility that a third party or independent candidate may run and draw votes away from the Democratic candidate in battleground states.

I also take equally seriously the reality that Americans have soured on the American-led rules-based international order. When they respond to questions from a public opinion pollster, they might respond that they still support that international order. But when Americans actually vote, tens of millions of them choose candidates who no longer have a firm attachment to that world order. Moreover, their preferences are reinforced by the tens of millions of Americans who are eligible to vote, but routinely choose not to.

Given this shift in American attitudes, in this book I have tried to sketch out the logical consequences of what would happen if an America First conservative nationalist returned to the White House and finished what Trump had begun in American foreign policy in 2017. The sketch is broadly drawn, and the geostrategic transform-ations I have bruited in Chapters 4 and 5 would likely be slow to unfold. But the logic of America First, when combined with the significant shifts in American politics, makes such transformations a distinct possibility.

Canadians need to start to taking the shifts in global politics that are underway — the assaults on the American-led international order by the People's Republic of China and the Russian Federation, and the profound shifts in American politics — more seriously. Unfortunately, the American world that Canadians lived in for the eight decades after the Second World War was so safe, so secure, and so comfortable that it led to a growing complacency about geopolitics, a complacency encouraged by the tendency of political leaders to urge Canadians to think of geopolitics as an ugly and "un-Canadian" term. Ideally, Canada's political leaders, along the entire political spectrum, will come to recognize that it would now be useful to start a conversation with Canadians about where we are in the world, particularly if the tectonic plates of global politics shift and leave us all alone to cope with America.

But coping with America, as Holmes wisely reminded us, "is and always has been an essential ingredient of being Canadian. It has formed us just as being an island formed Britain."[4] Canadians have always managed to find ways of dealing with the often unpredictable cycles of American politics, and the turn in American politics and foreign policy that resulted in — and from — the election of Donald J. Trump in 2016 was no different. If an America First president returns to the White House, backed by a Republican Party that is anti-democratic, illiberal, authoritarian, racist, nativist, and protectionist, Canadians will surely find Holmes's "new terms of agreement" — even if it means that Canada may eventually be all alone in the world with the Americans.

But I recognize that it is also possible that completely new "terms of agreement" may not be necessary. It is possible that American voters will prove Holmes right by continuing the trend that began in the midterms in 2022 and electing a Democratic president who is committed to the maintenance of both American leadership and the unity of the geostrategic West. Or it is possible that we may get to that result by another route: if Trump fails to secure the GOP nomination and, in a snit, runs as an independent, taking his MAGA cult with him, and severely splitting the Republican vote, resulting in a Democratic win. It is even possible — though it is a much longer shot — that Republicans voters and donors to the Republican Party, as they survey the wreckage produced by their long embrace of Trump and MAGA world, will have a collective damascene moment, and decide that they no longer wish to support a party that suffered such a dramatic "descent into madness," as *New York Times* writer Robert Draper so accurately put it.[5] Their collective decisions may result in the fever finally breaking, purging the party of its MAGA extremists, and in the process producing a presidential candidate who will reject America First and instead embrace a more traditional view of American global leadership.

In other words, it may turn out that the American world that has done so well for Canadians still has some life left in it after all.

ACKNOWLEDGEMENTS

This book has a highly specific origin. It began with a lecture given by a colleague and friend, Roland Paris, director of the Graduate School of Public and International Affairs at the University of Ottawa. In June 2019 Roland gave a keynote address at the annual meetings of the Canadian Political Science Association in Vancouver. His address, entitled "Canada alone? Surviving in a meaner world," provided a wide-ranging and thought-provoking *tour d'horizon* of the challenges facing Canada and Canadian foreign policy as a result not only of the rise of Donald J. Trump in the United States, but the transformation of the geopolitical environment with the rise of an increasingly assertive China; the impact of technology; the declining confidence in liberal democracy; and the challenges to the rules-based international order. Roland's conclusions were generally hopeful and optimistic. He answered the question posed in the title by suggesting that while the world was indeed a meaner place, Canada was not alone in the world, but could — and should — work with other states to buttress the international order, to protect each other from attacks by authoritarian states, and to use Canada's well-established capacity for establishing diverse coalitions of states to address global problems.

But his title, and its question mark, lingered with me. For looking at the effects of Trump's first two and a half years in office, and the sustained assaults on the American-led international order, I was not entirely convinced that it would be possible to repair that order if Trump continued to alienate the global network of friends and allies that were so crucial to the success of that order. And what would happen to Canada if that order was fully abandoned should Trump be re-elected, or another America First Republican elected as president? I decided to explore Roland's question using a longer, and more speculative, horizon. This book is the result. I would thus like to acknowledge Roland and thank him for giving me the idea of speculating on what might happen to Canada's foreign policy if an America First Republican president were to continue the sustained attacks on the American-led rules-based international order that Trump had started in 2017. I also thank him for providing the title of this book. It might be stripped of his question mark, but I use it as this book's title in homage to the question he first posed in 2019.

I was fortunate enough to be able to test some of the ideas developed in this book in public presentations in the last three years. To Christopher Kirkey, director of the Center for the Study of Canada at the State University of New York, Plattsburgh, my thanks for inviting me to give a keynote lecture at the annual meetings of the Association for Canadian Studies in the United States in Montréal in November 2019 on my reflections on the kind of world that Canada would face should Trump be re-elected. Colleagues at the meetings of the Nordic Association of Canadian Studies in Aarhus, Denmark, in August 2022 provided numerous very helpful suggestions on a paper I delivered there. Brian Bow, director of the Centre for the Study of Security and Development at Dalhousie University, was kind enough to arrange a seminar there in October 2022, and I very much appreciate all the feedback and ideas I received.

ACKNOWLEDGEMENTS

I am particularly grateful to the large number of colleagues who helped me in various ways as I sought to answer Roland's question: Rob Ayson, Kiran Banerjee, Margaret Biggs, Jean-Christophe Boucher, Ann Capling, Andrew Carr, Michael Collins, David Haglund, Fen Hampson, Frank Harvey, Thomas Juneau, Stéphanie Martel, Justin Massie, David Mulroney, Stuart MacKay, Stephen Nagy, Emma Shortis, Denis Stairs, and Robert Wolfe. And kudos to Sabrina Hoque and Sean Clark, who correctly anticipated the enduring relevance of Fareed Zakaria's post-American world more than a decade ago.

I would also like to thank the team at Dundurn for turning an idea into a book. Kathryn Lane, Dundurn's associate publisher, was an enthusiastic supporter from the outset. Karen Alexiou deserves a big shout-out for a wonderfully cheeky and imaginative cover. To the readers engaged by Dundurn, my thanks for all the suggestions that helped improve the final manuscript. My appreciation to Erin Pinksen, my project editor, for keeping things on track, and to Rajdeep Singh and Alyssa Boyden, my publicists at Dundurn, for all that they did — and will do — for the book. Finally, all authors invariably owe a major debt to their editors. I am no exception; I was hugely fortunate that Dundurn engaged Carrie Gleason as my editor. She has an extraordinary eye for the tics, inelegancies, repetition, slips, errors, non sequiturs, and gaps in logic that mar good writing, but she has a merciful tolerance for stylistic idiosyncrasies. Thanks, Carrie, for making me appear to be a much better writer than I actually am!

Finally, I want to acknowledge the contribution to this book of what has come to be known derisively in some quarters as the "mainstream media." Since 2015 the media has been widely criticized, particularly by those on the right in the United States, for how it presents the news. Donald J. Trump routinely calls the media "enemies of the people." He denigrates it as "fake news" and urges that those who work for the media be arrested or jailed. He encourages his MAGA followers not only to diss the media but also to openly threaten reporters, journalists, photographers, and videographers covering him. The parallels with Nazi Germany, where the media was routinely trashed as *die Lügenpresse* (the lying press), are simply too close for comfort. But this book would not have been possible without the coverage provided by that huge network of professionals who seek to provide chronicles, analyses, and commentaries on politics, accompanied by the videos and photographs that are so integral to the news. Some of their contributions will be acknowledged in the notes that follow; much of their work, however, will be neither visible nor acknowledged, the result of my decision to avoid footnoting many of the events, facts, and quotations whose veracity can be readily established with any search engine. But that invisibility in no way diminishes the debt that we owe all those professionals who work hard to maintain the free press that is so critical for a liberal democracy.

KRN
Howe Island, Ontario
March 2023

NOTES

Prologue

1   Anne Hidalgo (@Anne_Hidalgo), Twitter post, November 7, 2020, 11:40 a.m., Twitter, twitter.com/anne_hidalgo/status /1325115998966607873. For the relieved reactions of world leaders, see Mark Landler, "Biden victory brings sighs of relief overseas," *New York Times*, November 7, 2020, nytimes.com/2020/11/07/world /americas/biden-international-reaction.html.

2   Aaron Wherry, *Promise and Peril: Justin Trudeau in Power* (Toronto: HarperCollins, 2019), 154.

3   "Statement by the Prime Minister of Canada on the result of the U.S. presidential election," Ottawa, November 7, 2020, pm.gc.ca/en /news/statements/2020/11/07/statement-prime-minister-canada -result-us-presidential-election.

4   "Remarks by President Biden and Prime Minister Trudeau of Canada before virtual bilateral meeting," February 23, 2021, *U.S. Embassy & Consulates in Canada,* ca.usembassy.gov/remarks-by -president-biden-and-prime-minister-trudeau-of-canada-before -virtual-bilateral-meeting-february-23-2021/.

5   Aaron Wherry, "Enjoy this new normal in Canada-U.S. relations while it lasts," *CBC News*, February 24, 2021, cbc.ca/news/politics /trudeau-biden-bilateral-meeting-wherry-1.5925163.

Introduction

1 Colin Dueck, a political scientist at George Mason University and foreign policy adviser to several Republican presidential campaigns, has written extensively on Republican foreign policy. See Colin Dueck, *Hard Line: The Republican Party and U.S. Foreign Policy since World War II* (Princeton: Princeton University Press, 2011); also Dueck, *Age of Iron: On Conservative Nationalism* (New York: Oxford University Press, 2020). The names he gives the various traditions he identifies evolved over time: the conservative-nationalist tradition is drawn from *Age of Iron*.

2 The foreign minister was Lloyd Axworthy in a speech he gave in Washington in March 1996. Kim Richard Nossal, "'Without regard to the interests of others': Canada and American unilateralism in the post–Cold War era," *American Review of Canadian Studies* 27, no. 2 (1997): 179–97, doi.org/10.1080/02722019709481496.

3 David Rothkopf, *American Resistance: The Inside Story of How the Deep State Saved the Nation* (New York: Hachette Book Group/PublicAffairs, 2022).

4 Fareed Zakaria, *The Post-American World* (New York: W.W. Norton, 2008; updated 2009; updated and expanded as Release 2.0, 2011).

1. Canada's American World

1 Joseph S. Nye, Jr., "The rise and fall of American hegemony from Wilson to Trump," *International Affairs* 95, no. 1 (2019): 63–80, quotation at 72, doi.org/10.1093/ia/iiy212.

2 G. John Ikenberry, "The end of liberal international order?" *International Affairs* 94, no. 1 (2018): 7–23, doi.org/10.1093/ia/iix241.

3 A particularly problematic definition was the "civilizational" definition proffered by political scientist Samuel Huntington in *The Clash of Civilizations and the Remaking of World Order* (New York: Simon & Schuster, 1996). Huntington argued that the most important divisions in world politics are not nation-states, but "civilizations," and that world politics is about conflict between those "civilizations." While his "clash of civilizations" thesis continues to be periodically dredged up to try to explain

current events — it was most recently resuscitated to explain the Russian invasion of Ukraine — the book attracted widespread criticism when it first appeared, and continues to be widely criticized today. The title of a 2022 article by Nathan J. Robinson, a journalist and commentator, conveys a not uncommon view: "The 'clash of civilizations' thesis is still ignorant nonsense," *Current Affairs*, March 31, 2022, currentaffairs.org/2022/03/the -clash-of-civilizations-thesis-is-still-ignorant-nonsense.

4   Christopher S. Browning and Marko Lehti, "Introduction: New tensions in a troubled partnership," in Christopher S, Browning and Marko Lehti, eds., *The Struggle for the West: A Divided and Contested Legacy* (New York: Routledge, 2010), 18.

5   According to *The Economist*'s "democracy index," ten NATO members are "full democracies" and twenty-one are "flawed democracies." Türkiye, discussed more fully below, is the only NATO member ranked as a "hybrid regime." Economist Intelligence Unit, *Democracy Index, 2021: The China Challenge*, Table 2, 12–16, eiu.com/n/campaigns/democracy-index-2021/.

6   There is a counter-argument: Seth J. Frantzman, "Terra incognita: Israel is not a Western country, and never has been," *Jerusalem Post*, May 7, 2017, jpost.com/opinion/terra-incognita-israel-is-not-a -western-country-and-never-has-been-490048.

7   For example, Richard Fadden, former director of the Canadian Security Intelligence Service, includes Taiwan in his definition of the West: "2020 and beyond: Where does Canada fit?," Vimy Award Acceptance Speech, CDA Institute, Ottawa, November 12, 2019, cdainstitute.ca/richard-fadden-vimy-award-acceptance -speech-2020-and-beyond-where-does-canada-fit.

8   Richard Haass and David Sacks, "American support for Taiwan must be unambiguous," *Foreign Affairs*, September 2, 2020, foreignaffairs.com/articles/united-states/american-support-taiwan -must-be-unambiguous.

9   J.L. Granatstein, *Yankee Go Home? Canadians and Anti-Americanism* (Toronto: HarperCollins, 1997); Kim Richard Nossal, "Anti-Americanism in Canada," in Brendon O'Connor, ed., *Anti-Americanism: History, Causes, and Themes, vol. 3: Comparative Perspectives* (Oxford: Greenwood World Publishing, 2007), 59–76.

10   Michael C. Webb and Stephen D. Krasner, "Hegemonic stability theory: An empirical assessment," *Review of International Studies* 15, no. 2 (1989): 183–98, jstor.org/stable/20097178. The best

critique of hegemonic stability theory remains Isabelle Grunberg, "Exploring the 'myth' of hegemonic stability," *International Organization* 44, no. 4 (1990): 431–77, jstor.org/stable/2706850.

11 Mustafa Kutlay and Ziya Öniş, "Turkish foreign policy in a post-western order: Strategic autonomy or new forms of dependence?," *International Affairs* 97, no. 4 (2021): 1085–1104, doi.org/10.1093/ia /iiab094.

12 Freedom House rates Türkiye as "not free," with a score of 32/100. See freedomhouse.org/country/turkey/freedom-world/2022. On *The Economist*'s "democracy index," Türkiye has a score of just 4.35, the lowest of all Western countries. *Democracy Index, 2021*, Appendix, 68.

13 Unlike a free trade area, in which countries agree to remove barriers to trade between themselves but maintain their own separate trade policies, in a customs union, barriers to trade among member countries are removed and all members adopt a unified customs policy toward non-member countries. Türkiye and the European Union entered into a customs union in 1995, creating a common external tariff and eliminating customs restrictions to all goods except agriculture, services, and public procurement.

14 The best survey of Canada's contribution remains the two-volume history by John W. Holmes: *The Shaping of Peace: Canada and the Search for World Order, 1943–1957* (Toronto: University of Toronto Press, 1979, 1982).

15 Tom Keating, *Canada and World Order: The Multilateralist Tradition in Canadian Foreign Policy*, 3rd ed. (Toronto: Oxford University Press, 2013).

16 Renato Ruggiero, "The road ahead: International trade policy in the era of the WTO," Fourth Sylvia Ostry Lecture, Ottawa, May 28, 1996, wto.org/english/news_e/pres96_e/pr049_e.htm.

17 Canada, National Defence, *Strong, Secure, Engaged: Canada's Defence Policy* (Ottawa: Government of Canada, 2017), canada.ca /content/dam/dnd-mdn/documents/reports/2018/strong-secure -engaged/canada-defence-policy-report.pdf

18 Joel S. Sokolsky, "Realism Canadian style: National security policy and the Chrétien legacy," *Policy Matters* 5, no. 2 (2004): 11, irpp.org /wp-content/uploads/assets/pmvol5no2.pdf.

19 Lorraine Eden and Fen Osler Hampson, "Clubs are trump: The formation of international regimes in the absence of a hegemon," in J. Rogers Hollingsworth and Robert Boyer, eds., *Contemporary*

Capitalism: The Embeddedness of Institutions (New York: Cambridge University Press, 1999), 361–94.

20 Canada, Secretary of State for External Affairs, *Foreign Policy for Canadians* (Ottawa: Supply and Services Canada, 1970), Pacific booklet, 10–13.

21 Ed Fast, "Address by Minister Fast to the 18th Annual Conference of Montreal," Montréal, June 13, 2012, canada.ca/en/news/archive /2012/06/address-minister-fast-18th-annual-conference-montreal .html.

22 Michael Hart, "Canada discovers its vocation as a nation of the Americas," in Fen Osler Hampson and Christopher J. Maule, eds., *Canada Among Nations, 1990–91: After the Cold War* (Ottawa: Carleton University Press, 1991), 83–107, quotation at 83.

23 Environics Institute, *Canada's World Survey 2018: Final Report*, April 2018, esp. 24, environicsinstitute.org/docs/default-source /project-documents/canada's-world-2018-survey/canada's-world -survey-2018---final-report.pdf; Steven Chase, "Canadian opinions of the U.S. at lowest in nearly 40 years, polling program shows," *Globe and Mail*, October 15, 2020, theglobeandmail.com/politics /article-canadian-opinions-of-the-us-at-lowest-in-nearly-40-years -polling/; Macdonald-Laurier Institute, *Canada's Role in the World: Annual Foreign Policy and International Affairs Survey*, January 2022, 34–35, macdonaldlaurier.ca/mli-files/pdf/Canada_Role _in_the_World_Jan_2022.pdf.

24 Pew Research Center, "International attitudes toward the U.S., NATO and Russia in a time of crisis," June 22, 2022, pewresearch.org/global/wp-content/uploads/sites/2/2022/06/PG _2022.07.22_U.S.-Image_FINAL.pdf.

25 Environics Institute, *Canada's World Survey 2018*, 15; Steven Chase, "Eight out of 10 Canadians say China has negative influence on world affairs: Poll," *Globe and Mail*, November 7, 2022, theglobeandmail.com/politics/article-eight-out-of-10-canadians -say-china-has-negative-influence-on-world/.

26 Lloyd Axworthy, *Navigating a New World: Canada's Global Future* (Toronto: Random House Canada, 2003), 407.

27 Kim Richard Nossal, "Rethinking the security imaginary: Canadian security and the case of Afghanistan," in Bruno Charbonneau and Wayne S. Cox, eds., *Locating Global Order: American Power and Canadian Security after 9/11* (Vancouver: UBC Press, 2010), 107–25, nossalk.files.wordpress.com/2021/05

/nossal_2010_security-imaginary-1.pdf; the electoral connection is explored in Kim Richard Nossal, "A thermostatic dynamic? Electoral outcomes and anti-Americanism in Canada," in Richard A. Higgott and Ivona Malbašić, eds., *The Political Consequences of Anti-Americanism* (New York: Routledge, 2008), 129–41, nossalk.files .wordpress.com/2021/10/nossal_2008_thermostatic.pdf.

28   Canada, Parliament, House of Commons, *Debates*, 37th Parl., 2nd sess., no. 084, April 3, 2003, 10h55, ourcommons.ca /DocumentViewer/en/37-2/house/sitting-84/hansard.

29   Duane Bratt, "Stephen Harper and the politics of Canada-US relations," in Peter McKenna, ed., *Harper's World: The Politicization of Canadian Foreign Policy, 2006–2015* (Toronto: University of Toronto Press, 2022), 165–88, quotation at 168.

30   Mike Blanchfield, *Swingback: Getting Along in the World with Harper and Trudeau* (Montreal and Kingston: McGill-Queen's University Press, 2017), 224–26.

31   Chrystia Freeland, "Address by Minister Freeland on Canada's foreign policy priorities," Ottawa, June 6, 2017, canada.ca/en /global-affairs/news/2017/06/address_by_ ministerfreelandoncanadasforeignpolicypriorities.html.

32   Chrystia Freeland, "Address by Minister Freeland when receiving Foreign Policy's Diplomat of the Year Award," Washington, DC, June 13, 2018, canada.ca/en/global-affairs/news/2018/06/address -by-minister-freeland-when-receiving-foreign-policys-diplomat-of -the-year-award.html.

2. The Assault on the American World

1   Charles Krauthammer, "The unipolar moment," *Washington Post*, July 20, 1990, washingtonpost.com/archive/opinions/1990/07/20 /the-unipolar-moment/62867add-2fe9-493f-a0c9-4bfba1ec23bd/.

2   Kim Richard Nossal, "Lonely superpower or unapologetic hyperpower: Analyzing American power in the post–Cold War era," South African Political Studies Association conference, Saldanha, Western Cape, June 29–July 2, 1999, nossalk.files.wordpress.com /2021/01/nossal_1999_hyperpower.pdf.

3   In 1990 Deng issued what became known as his "24-character strategy" to guide future Chinese leaders. Four of those characters advised that in international affairs China should "韬光养晦" [tāo

guāng yǎng huì], literally "hide brightness, nourish obscurity." However, worried that "hide capabilities" would come across as China being deceptive, the official Chinese translation was "keep a low profile, bide your time."

4   Charles Krauthammer, "The unipolar moment," *Foreign Affairs* 70, no. 1, America and the World (1990/91): 23–33, quotation at 23–24, jstor.org/stable/20044692.

5   United States, Senate, Committee on Foreign Relations, *United States-China Relations in the Era of Globalization: Hearing before the Committee on Foreign Relations*, 110th Cong., 2nd sess., May 15, 2008, 31. By 2016 Richard Haass was arguing that the global order was fracturing: *A World in Disarray: American Foreign Policy and the Crisis of the Old Order* (New York: Penguin Press, 2017).

6   PBS, *Frontline*, "Putin's revenge (part one)," October 17, 2017, pbs.org /wgbh/frontline/documentary/putins-revenge/; transcript: pbs.org /wgbh/frontline/documentary/putins-revenge/transcript/.

7   Vladimir Vladimirovich Putin, "Speech and the following discussion at the Munich Conference on Security Policy," Munich, February 10, 2007, en.kremlin.ru/events/president/transcripts/24034.

8   David Shimer, *Rigged: America, Russia, and One Hundred Years of Covert Electoral Interference* (New York: Vintage, 2020); on the Mariupol plan, see Jim Rutenberg, "The untold story of 'Russiagate' and the road to war in Ukraine," *New York Times*, November 2, 2022, nytimes.com/2022/11/02/magazine/russiagate-paul-manafort -ukraine-war.html.

9   See the 2021 essay in which Putin sought to justify his policy toward Ukraine: V.V. Putin, "On the historical unity of Russians and Ukrainians," July 12, 2021, en.kremlin.ru/events/president/news/66181.

10   President of Russia, "Address by the President of the Russian Federation," Moscow, February 21, 2022, en.kremlin.ru/events /president/news/67828.

11   President of Russia, "Meeting with young entrepreneurs, engineers and scientists," St. Petersburg, June 9, 2022, en.kremlin.ru/events /president/news/68606.

12   Roland Paris, "The right to dominate: How old ideas about sovereignty pose new challenges for world order," *International Organization* 74, no. 3 (2020): 453–89, doi.org/10.1017/S0020818320000077.

13   Stephen N. Smith, "China's 'Major Country Diplomacy': Legitimation and foreign policy change," *Foreign Policy Analysis* 17, no. 2 (April 2021), doi.org/10.1093/fpa/orab002.

14   For an exploration of Xi's efforts to realize his strategic ambitions for China, see Elizabeth C. Economy, *The World According to China* (Cambridge, U.K.: Polity Press, 2022).

15   Atlantic Council Digital Forensic Research Lab, "Chinese discourse power: China's use of information manipulation in regional and global competition," December 2020, ftn 5, atlanticcouncil.org/wp -content/uploads/2020/12/China-Discouse-Power-FINAL.pdf.

16   See imdb.com/title/tt7131870/; the tag line in Chinese is "犯我中华者 虽远必诛!"

17   Cited in Peter Martin, *China's Civilian Army: The Making of Wolf Warrior Diplomacy* (New York: Oxford University Press, 2021), 222.

18   According to the CPC's Central Commission for Disciplinary Inspection, in 2018, of 1,335 "fugitives" returned to China, seventeen were returned via extradition; in 2021, 1,273 "fugitives" were returned with twenty-two captured through INTERPOL red notices. "1,273 fugitives returned to China last year to face justice," *Global Times*, February 25, 2022, globaltimes.cn/page /202202/1253173.shtml.

19   On Sky Net and Fox Hunt, see the investigative reports of Safeguard Defenders, a European human rights NGO: safeguarddefenders .com/en, particularly "China announces expansion of Sky Net and long-arm policing," March 28, 2022; *110 Overseas: Chinese Transnational Policing Gone Wild*, September 2022.

20   Gerry Groot, "The rise and rise of the United Front Work Department under Xi," *China Brief* 18, no. 7 (April 30, 2018), jamestown.org/program/the-rise-and-rise-of-the-united-front-work -department-under-xi/.

21   Stephanie Carvin, *Stand on Guard: Reassessing Threats to Canada's National Security* (Toronto: University of Toronto Press, 2021), esp. 202–19; Jonathan Manthorpe, *Claws of the Panda: Beijing's Campaign of Influence and Intimidation in Canada* (Toronto: Cormorant Books, 2019).

22   Sam Cooper, "Canadian intelligence warned PM Trudeau that China covertly funded 2019 election candidates," Global News, November 7, 2022, globalnews.ca/news/9253386/canadian-intelligence -warned-pm-trudeau-that-china-covertly-funded-2019-election -candidates-sources/. While Cooper claimed that CSIS warned Trudeau that China had funded eleven candidates, the national security adviser, Jody Thomas, testified to a parliamentary committee that the news stories about funding "are just that — news stories.

I'll just say it — we've not seen money going to eleven candidates, period." Murray Brewster, "PM's national security adviser says she's seen 'no evidence' of foreign funding to federal election candidates," *CBC News*, December 8, 2022, cbc.ca/news/politics /jody-thomas-china-election-interference-1.6679443.

23 Clive Hamilton, *Silent Invasion: China's Influence in Australia* (Richmond, Au.: Hardie Grant Books, 2018); Alex Joske, "The Party speaks for you: Foreign interference and the Chinese Communist Party's united front system," *Australian Strategic Policy Institute*, June 9, 2020, aspi.org.au/report/party-speaks-you; Abhijnan Rej, "Australia combats China's interference amid deep discord in relations," *The Diplomat*, November 9, 2020, thediplomat.com/2020/11/australia-combats-chinas-interference -amid-deep-discord-in-relations/.

24 Mike Blanchfield and Fen Osler Hampson, *The Two Michaels: Innocent Canadian Captives and High Stakes Espionage in the US– China Cyber War* (Toronto: Sutherland House, 2021).

25 Michael Gui Minhai (no relation to the ambassador) was a Swedish citizen who ran a bookstore in Hong Kong, where one could buy lurid gossipy tabloid-style books critical of the Chinese leadership with titles like *Secrets of Wives of Chinese Communist Party Officials* and *The General Secretary's Eight Love Stories* — all banned in mainland China. In 2015 Gui was kidnapped while on vacation in Thailand and rendered to China, where he was put on trial and sentenced to ten years in prison on espionage charges.

26 Laura Silver, Christine Huang, and Laura Clancy, "How global public opinion of China has shifted in the Xi era," Pew Research Center, September 28, 2022, pewresearch.org/global/2022/09/28 /how-global-public-opinion-of-china-has-shifted-in-the-xi-era/.

27 In the past Beijing has also translated the phrase as "community of common destiny for humankind" and "community of shared future for humankind."

28 Xi Jinping, "Report to the 20th National Congress of the Communist Party of China," October 16, 2022, english.www.gov.cn /2022special/20thcpccongress/.

29 Kevin Rudd, "The world according to Xi Jinping," *Foreign Affairs* 101, no. 6 (2022): 8–21, quotation at 10, foreignaffairs.com/china /world-according-xi-jinping-china-ideologue-kevin-rudd.

30 Willy Wo-Lap Lam, "The 20th Party Congress: Xi Jinping exerts overwhelming control over personnel, but offers no clues on

reviving the economy," *China Brief* 22, no. 20 (November 3, 2022), jamestown.org/program/the-20th-party-congress-xi-jinping-exerts-overwhelming-control-over-personnel-but-offers-no-clues-on-reviving-the-economy/.

31 This ugly portmanteau is a play on the various ways that supply chains can be organized. "Off-shoring" was first used in the 1980s to describe the transfer of production and supply chains to other countries to take advantage of lower labour costs; "on-shoring" (or "reshoring") was production that was brought "back home," so that supply chains were sourced within a single country's borders. Friend-shoring is the creation of supply chains with dependable friends and allies as a way of insulating a country from dependence on non-democratic states. A Trump official invented the term "allied-shoring" in 2019. The Biden administration altered it to "friend-shoring" or "ally-shoring." Peter Coy, "'Onshoring' is so last year. The new lingo is 'friend-shoring,'" *Bloomberg*, June 24, 2021, bloomberg.com/news/articles/2021-06-24/-onshoring-is-so-last-year-the-new-lingo-is-friend-shoring.

32 See, for example, Andrew Small, *No Limits: The Inside Story of China's War with the West* (London: C. Hurst & Co., 2022). It should be noted that the use of the word "war" in Small's subtitle is purely figurative, for unlike books like Ted Galen Carpenter's *America's Coming War with China* (New York: Palgrave Macmillan, 2005), David C. Gompert et al., *War with China: Thinking Through the Unthinkable* (Santa Monica, Calif.: RAND Corporation, 2016), or Graham T. Allison, *Destined For War: Can America and China Escape Thucydides's Trap?* (New York: Houghton Mifflin Harcourt, 2017), this book is not about war but about the growing *systemic conflict* between China and the West.

33 Rush Doshi, *The Long Game: China's Grand Strategy to Displace American Order* (New York: Oxford University Press, 2021).

34 John Pomfret, "U.S. takes a tougher tone with China," *Washington Post*, July 30, 2010, washingtonpost.com/wp-dyn/content/article/2010/07/29/AR2010072906416.html.

35 For a fuller discussion of how China sees the world, see Paris, "Right to dominate," 17–22, and Elizabeth C. Economy, "History with Chinese characteristics," *Foreign Affairs* 96, no. 4 (2017), 141–48, jstor.org/stable/44823900.

36 Stephanie Grisham, *I'll Take Your Questions Now: What I Saw at the Trump White House* (New York: HarperCollins Publishers, 2021).

37　The signal unusualness of Trump's interpersonal relationships is explored in Dan P. McAdams, *The Strange Case of Donald J. Trump: A Psychological Reckoning* (New York: Oxford University Press, 2020).

38　Daniel W. Drezner, *The Toddler-in-Chief: What Donald Trump Teaches Us About the Modern Presidency* (Chicago: University of Chicago Press, 2020), 179, 63.

39　United States, White House, "Inaugural address," Washington, DC, January 20, 2017, trumpwhitehouse.archives.gov/briefings -statements/the-inaugural-address.

40　Maggie Haberman, *Confidence Man: The Making of Donald Trump and the Breaking of America* (New York: Penguin Press, 2022), 310.

41　Anonymous [Miles Taylor], *A Warning* (New York: Grand Central Publishing, 2019).

42　John Wagner, "Trump says defending tiny NATO ally Montenegro could lead to World War III," *Washington Post*, July 18, 2018, washingtonpost.com/politics/trump-says-defending-tiny-nato-ally -montenegro-could-lead-to-world-war-iii/2018/07/18/f7a09276 -8a80-11e8-8aea-86e88ae760d8_story.html; YouTube video clip at youtube.com/watch?v=wqVg8byadj0, 1:49.

43　Brooks Spector, "Trump to Zelensky on Ukraine: Nice country you have there, it would be a shame if something happened to it," *Daily Maverick*, Johannesburg, September 26, 2019, dailymaverick.co.za /article/2019-09-26-trump-to-zelensky-on-ukraine-nice-country -you-have-there-it-would-be-a-shame-if-something-happened-to-it/.

44　"Statement by President Trump on the Paris Climate Accord," Washington, DC, June 1, 2017, trumpwhitehouse.archives.gov /briefings-statements/statement-president-trump-paris-climate-accord/.

45　Wendy Sherman, "How we got the Iran deal, and why we'll miss it," *Foreign Affairs* (September/October, 2018), foreignaffairs.com/united -states/how-we-got-iran-deal.

46　Kristen Hopewell, "When the hegemon goes rogue: Leadership amid the US assault on the liberal trading order," *International Affairs* 97, no. 4 (2021): 1025–43, doi.org/10.1093/ia/iiab073.

47　John Bolton, *The Room Where It Happened: A White House Memoir* (New York: Simon & Schuster, 2020), 309–13.

48　Abram C. Van Engen, *City on a Hill: A History of American Exceptionalism* (New Haven: Yale University Press, 2020).

49　Shana Kushner Gadarian, Sara Wallace Goodman, and Thomas B. Pepinsky, *Pandemic Politics: The Deadly Toll of Partisanship in the Age of COVID* (Princeton: Princeton University Press, 2022).

50 For 692 pages of unambiguous evidence that Trump and a number
of his advisers and associates planned and executed an attempted
self-coup, see United States, House of Representatives, *Final Report
of the Select Committee to Investigate the January 6th Attack on the
United States Capitol*, December 2022, published as *The January
6th Report*, with a foreword by Ari Melber (New York: Harper,
2022).

51 Haberman, *Confidence Man*, 309–10.

52 Philip Rucker and Carol Leonnig, *A Very Stable Genius: Donald J.
Trump's Testing of America* (New York: Penguin Press, 2020), 133.

53 Conrad Black, *Donald J. Trump: A President Like No Other*
(Washington, DC: Regnery Publishing, 2018).

3. Whither American Politics?

1 "Stop the Steal" was both an organization designed to raise money
for Trump and a political movement. It was originally launched
in 2016 by Roger Stone, a Trump adviser, as a means to be able to
claim that any electoral loss by Trump was as a result of fraud. In
2020 it was run by another Trump ally, Ali Alexander, and was
used as a fundraising campaign by Trump and formed part of the
effort to overturn the 2020 election. But it also became a political
movement as "Stop the Steal" groups were formed around the
United States to protest the election results.

2 Barton Gellman, "Trump's next coup has already begun," *The Atlantic*,
December 6, 2021, theatlantic.com/magazine/archive/2022/01
/january-6-insurrection-trump-coup-2024-election/620843/.

3 States United Democracy Center, *A Democracy Crisis in the
Making: How State Legislatures are Politicizing, Criminalizing,
and Interfering with Election Administration*, April 22, 2021,
statesuniteddemocracy.org/wp-content/uploads/2021/04/FINAL
-Democracy-Crisis-Report-April-21.pdf.

4 According to Media Matters for America, a not-for-profit monitor
of conservative U.S. media, support for QAnon can range from
open and diehard adherence to those who signal implicit support
by using the hashtag #WWG1WGA or the letter Q. Some of the
supporters identified by Media Matters have since tried to disavow
their earlier embrace of the conspiracy. Alex Kaplan, "Here are
the QAnon supporters running for Congress in 2022," *Media*

Matters, June 2, 2021, mediamatters.org/qanon-conspiracy-theory /here-are-qanon-supporters-running-congress-2022.

5   "Remarks by President Biden in press conference," Washington, DC, November 9, 2022, whitehouse.gov/briefing-room/speeches-remarks /2022/11/09/remarks-by-president-biden-in-press-conference-8/; David Brooks, "The fever is breaking," *New York Times,* November 10, 2022, nytimes.com/2022/11/10/opinion/the-fever-is-breaking .html; Fareed Zakaria, "Has the Republican fever broken?" *Washington Post,* November 10, 2022, washingtonpost.com/opinions /2022/11/10/republican-midterms-undermine-trump-dominance/.

6   Tom Nichols, "Democracy's Dunkirk," *The Atlantic,* November 18, 2022, theatlantic.com/newsletters/archive/2022/11/democracys -dunkirk/672187/.

7   Barton Gellman, "How six states could overturn the 2024 election," *The Atlantic,* July 29, 2022, theatlantic.com/ideas/archive/2022/07 /moore-harper-scotus-independent-state-legislature-election-power /670992/.

8   Eli J. Finkel, et al., "Political sectarianism in America: A poisonous cocktail of othering, aversion, and moralization poses a threat to democracy," *Science* 370, no. 6516 (2020), 533–46, doi.org/10.1126 /SCIENCE.ABE1715. See also Shanto Iyengar, Yphtach Lelkes, Matthew Levendusky, Neil Malhotra, and Sean J. Westwood, "The origins and consequences of affective polarization in the United States," *Annual Review of Political Science* 22 (2019): 129–46, doi.org /10.1146/annurev-polisci-051117-073034.

9   In 2022 Democrats controlled seventeen of forty-nine legislatures; in only fourteen of forty-nine states did Democrats hold both legislative chambers and the governorship. (Note that Nebraska is normally excluded from these calculations because the Nebraska Legislature is not only unicameral, but also "non-partisan" — in other words, the party affiliations of its members are not officially recognized.) For details, see National Conference of State Legislatures, "State partisan composition," June 1, 2022, ncsl.org /research/about-state-legislatures/partisan-composition.aspx.

10   The best exploration of the submissiveness of elected Republicans to Trump is Mark Leibovich, *Thank You for Your Servitude: Donald Trump's Washington and the Price of Submission* (New York: Penguin Press, 2022).

11   Of the ten House Republicans who voted to impeach Trump in 2021, only Dan Newhouse (R-Wash.) and David Valadao (R-Calif.)

made it back to Congress in 2023. Four decided to retire. The remaining four who sought re-election — Liz Cheney (R-Wyo.), Jaime Herrera Beutler (R-Wash.), Peter Meijer (R-Mich.), and Tom Rice (R-S.C.) — were all censured by their local Republican party organizations and primaried before the general election. Of the seven GOP senators who voted to convict Trump, two chose not to run again in 2022; three were not due for re-election until 2026; and one, Mitt Romney (R-Utah), was not up for re-election until 2024. Lisa Murkowski of Alaska was the only one who had to face the voters in the 2022 midterms. Although the Alaska Republican Party censured her, called for her resignation, and tried to primary her, Murkowski was able to secure re-election, partly because she has an independent base of support in the state, and partly because Alaska has an unusual primary system that makes it virtually impossible to primary a candidate. In other states all parties run a separate slate of primary candidates to determine the party's candidate in the general election. Alaska has a "non-partisan pick one primary election" system: all candidates from all parties are listed on a single ballot. Voters, regardless of their party registration, get one vote with the top four candidates, regardless of party, proceeding to the general election to determine which one of the four finalists will go to Congress.

12 The phrase was originally used by Tea Party critics of the "establishment" Republicans. Today it is used, most devastatingly by Rick Wilson, a former GOP strategist and author, to describe those elected Republicans who enable Trump and the MAGA Republicans. See, for example, Rick Wilson, "The three rules MAGA Republicans live by," *Lincoln Project*, n.d. [October, 2022], lincolnproject.us/three-rules-maga-republicans/.

13 Jennifer Rubin, "Republicans are still afraid of Trump," *Washington Post*, November 22, 2022, washingtonpost.com/opinions/2022/11/22/republicans-afraid-trump-presidential-contenders-2024/.

14 Jamelle Bouie, "Republican elites might be done with Trump, but he's not done with them," *New York Times*, November 12, 2022, nytimes.com/2022/11/12/opinion/trump-election-republican.html.

15 Greene was trying to criticize Nancy Pelosi, the Speaker of the House, for allegedly ordering the U.S. Capitol Police to enter the offices of Rep. Troy Nehls (R-Texas): "Now we have Nancy Pelosi's gazpacho police spying on members of Congress, spying on the legislative work that we do."

16   "Tracking which 2020 election deniers are winning, losing in the midterms," washingtonpost.com/politics/interactive/2022/election-deniers-midterms/.

17   Robert Draper, *Weapons of Mass Delusion: When the Republican Party Lost Its Mind* (New York: Penguin Press, 2022).

18   Steven Levitsky and Daniel Ziblatt, *How Democracies Die* (New York: Broadway Books, 2018), 21.

19   Klaus Larres, "Donald J. Trump: The authoritarian style in American politics," in Klaus Larres, ed., *Dictators and Autocrats: Securing Power across Global Politics* (New York: Routledge, 2021), 204–31, doi.org/10.4324/9781003100508-16.

20   YouTube video clip at youtube.com/watch?v=-jqeCgxRKD4; Charlie Sykes, "The right's lust for violence," *The Bulwark*, September 28, 2022, morningshots.thebulwark.com/p/the-rights-lust-for-violence.

21   See Sec. 171.208 (3) (b) of the Act: webservices.sos.state.tx.us/legbills/files/RS87/SB8.pdf; Sabrina Tavernise, "Citizens, not the state, will enforce new abortion law in Texas," *New York Times*, July 9, 2021, nytimes.com/2021/07/09/us/abortion-law-regulations-texas.html.

22   Margaret Atwood's novel, *The Handmaid's Tale* (1985), the five-season television series of the same name (2017–22), and a follow-up novel, *The Testaments* (2019), portray a future dystopian America following the overthrow of the United States and the establishment of a deeply patriarchal, fundamentalist, and totalitarian theocracy, the Republic of Gilead, in which women are forced into sexual servitude, not permitted to read or write or own property with their reproductive rights brutally suppressed. On the mirror between the Hulu TV series and contemporary efforts in the U.S. to control women's bodies, see Maria Cardona, "We cannot allow 'The Handmaid's Tale' to become reality TV," *The Hill*, May 17, 2019, thehill.com/opinion/civil-rights/444054-we-cannot-allow-the-handmaids-tale-to-become-reality-tv/.

23   David Corn, "Texas shows how Trumpism is becoming fascistic vigilantism," *This Land*, September 3, 2021, link.motherjones.com/public/24936287. In the series Lydia was an Aunt, a group of women responsible for training the Handmaids, overseeing births, and managing executions.

24   Andrew L. Whitehead and Samuel L. Perry, *Taking America Back For God: Christian Nationalism in the United States* (New York: Oxford University Press, 2020). For a primer see Philip

S. Gorski and Samuel L. Perry, *The Flag and the Cross: White Christian Nationalism and the Threat to American Democracy* (New York: Oxford University Press, 2022). For a full survey of American Christian nationalist attitudes, see "A Christian nation? Understanding the threat of Christian nationalism to American democracy and culture," *Public Religion Research Institute*, February 8, 2023, prri.org/research/a-christian-nation-understanding-the-threat-of-christian-nationalism-to-american-democracy-and-culture/.

25   Pew Research Center, "Faith and flag conservatives," pewresearch.org/politics/2021/11/09/faith-and-flag-conservatives/.

26   Maggie Haberman and Alan Feuer, "Trump's latest dinner guest: Nick Fuentes, White supremacist," *New York Times*, November 25, 2022, nytimes.com/2022/11/25/us/politics/trump-nick-fuentes-dinner.html.

27   Jonathan Rauch, "Trump's second term would look like this," *The Atlantic*, August 29, 2022, theatlantic.com/ideas/archive/2022/08/trump-2024-reelection-viktor-orban-hungary/671264/.

28   Stuart Stevens (@stuartpstevens), Twitter post, June 21, 2022, 6:02 p.m., twitter.com/stuartpstevens/status/1539368122360254465, emphasis added; Stuart Stevens, *It Was All a Lie: How the Republican Party Became Donald Trump* (New York: Vintage Books, 2021), xiii.

29   Since the late 1970s, LGBTQ+ members of the GOP have had an organization, Log Cabin Republicans (logcabin.org), to press for greater inclusivity within the party. The name is a reference to Abraham Lincoln, who was born in a log cabin and who sought to achieve equality. The impact of the Log Cabin Republicans, however, has been mixed. At the state level, particularly in red states, there is still considerable anti-LGBTQ+ sentiment. See, for example, Eric Neugeboren, "'We failed': Gay Republicans who fought for acceptance in Texas GOP see little progress," *Texas Tribune*, July 24, 2022, texastribune.org/2022/07/24/texas-log-cabin-republicans/.

30   Jacob K. Javits, "To preserve the two-party system," *New York Times Magazine*, October 27, 1963, 105.

31   Ian Haney López, *Dog Whistle Politics: How Coded Racial Appeals Have Reinvented Racism and Wrecked the Middle Class* (New York: Oxford University Press, 2014).

32   Christopher S. Parker and Matt A. Barreto, *Change They Can't Believe In: The Tea Party and Reactionary Politics in America* (Princeton: Princeton University Press, 2013).

33 With one notable exception: see how Sen. John McCain (R-Ariz.), who at the time was the GOP candidate for president, dealt with a case of anti-Obama racism at a town hall in Lakeville, Minnesota, during the 2008 election campaign: YouTube video clip at youtube.com /watch?v=JIjenjANqAk, August 10, 2008.

4. The Persistence of America First

1 Sarah Zhang, "Trump's most trusted adviser is his own gut," *The Atlantic*, January 13, 2019, theatlantic.com/politics/archive/2019/01 /trump-follows-his-gut/580084/; Eliza Collins, "Trump: I consult myself on foreign policy," *Politico*, March 16, 2016, politico.com /blogs/2016-gop-primary-live-updates-and-results/2016/03/trump -foreign-policy-adviser-220853.
2 Bob Woodward, *Rage* (New York: Simon & Schuster, 2020), 139.
3 David Brooks, "When the world is led by a child," *New York Times*, May 15, 2017, nytimes.com/2017/05/15/opinion/trump-classified-data .html.
4 Stephen M. Walt, "Trump's final foreign-policy report card," *Foreign Policy*, January 5, 2021, foreignpolicy.com/2021/01/05/trumps-final -foreign-policy-report-card/.
5 For the laugh-out-loud response of world leaders to Trump's hyperbolic claims about his administration's accomplishments — and Trump's own rattled reaction to being openly laughed at on the world stage — see *BBC News*, September 25, 2018, bbc.com/news /av/world-us-canada-45644975; see also Aaron Blake, "A brief history of world leaders laughing at Trump," *Washington Post*, December 4, 2019, washingtonpost.com/politics/2019/12/04/brief-history -world-leaders-laughing-trump/.
6 Kathryn Dunn Tenpas, "Crippling the capacity of the National Security Council," *Brookings Institution*, January 21, 2020, brookings.edu /blog/fixgov/2020/01/21/crippling-the-capacity-of-the-national -security-council/.
7 David Rothkopf, *American Resistance: The Inside Story of How the Deep State Saved the Nation* (New York: Hachette Book Group/ PublicAffairs, 2022).
8 On the "Schedule F" issue, see Jonathan Swan, "A radical plan for Trump's second term," *Axios*, July 22, 2022, axios.com/2022/07/22 /trump-2025-radical-plan-second-term.

9   Bob Woodward and Robert Costa, *Peril* (New York: Simon & Schuster, 2021), 414.

10 Arnold Schwarzenegger (@schwarzenegger), "President Trump, remember, America first," Instagram, July 16, 2018, instagram.com/p /BlT1xFMhUsx/?hl=en.

11 For a full list of Carlson's on-air comments about Russia, Putin, and Ukraine from December 2016 to March 2022, see Nikki McCann Ramirez et al., "Tucker Carlson's history of pro-Kremlin, anti-Ukraine propaganda," *Media Matters*, March 4, 2022, mediamatters. org/russias-invasion-ukraine/tucker-carlsons-history-pro-kremlin -anti-ukraine-propaganda.

12 *Tucker Carlson Tonight*, May 2, 2022, youtube.com/watch?v =wGvO8b-tiaM.

13 Daniel W. Drezner, "The awkward DeSantis straddle," *Drezner's World*, March 24, 2023, danieldrezner.substack.com/p/the-awkward -desantis-straddle.

14 Trump appears to be obsessed about being addressed as "sir," and invariably litters his storytelling with people addressing him as sir. For a (searchable) database of 469 of Trump's "sir stories," see Richie Lionell, "The *Sir* stories of President Trump," richielionell.github.io /president-trump-sir-stories/.

15 "Trump speaks at CPAC 2023 transcript," *Rev.com*, March 6, 2023, video embedded, rev.com/blog/transcripts/trump-speaks-at-cpac -2023-transcript; NATO story at 0:46:47–0:49:20.

16 John J. Mearsheimer, "Why the Ukraine crisis is the West's fault," *Foreign Affairs* 93, no. 5 (2014): 77–89, jstor.org/stable/24483306; Isaac Chotiner, "John Mearsheimer on Putin's ambitions after nine months of war," *New Yorker*, November 17, 2022, newyorker.com /news/q-and-a/john-mearsheimer-on-putins-ambitions-after-nine -months-of-war. For a good critique of Mearsheimer that places his argument in a broader theoretical context, see Nicholas Ross Smith and Grant Dawson, "Mearsheimer, realism, and the Ukraine war," *Analyse & Kritik* 44, no. 2 (2022): 175–200, degruyter.com /document/doi/10.1515/auk-2022-2023/html.

17 United States Senate, roll call vote 117th Congress, 2nd sess., August 3, 2022, www.senate.gov/legislative/LIS/roll_call_votes /vote1172/vote_117_2_00282.htm. Three senators missed the vote: John Cornyn (R-Texas) was isolating with COVID-19; Patrick Leahy (D-Vt.) was recovering from hip surgery; and Jeff Merkley (D-Ore.) was travelling to be with his dying mother. All three

indicated that had they been able to attend, they would have voted in favour.

18 United States, *National Security Strategy of the United States of America*, December 2017, 25, trumpwhitehouse.archives.gov/wp -content/uploads/2017/12/NSS-Final-12-18-2017-0905.pdf.

19 For a detailed timeline, see Norman Pearlstine, Priya Krishnakumar, and David Pierson, "The war against Huawei," *Los Angeles Times*, December 19, 2019, latimes.com/projects/la-fg-huawei-timeline/.

20 The best account of China policy during the Trump administration is Josh Rogin, *Chaos Under Heaven: Trump, Xi, and the Battle for the Twenty-First Century* (New York: Houghton Mifflin Harcourt, 2021).

21 Trump interview, "Sunday Morning Futures," Fox News, December 19, 2021, video.foxnews.com/v/6287646727001.

5. A Post-American World

1 When CBS Evening News anchor Jeff Glor asked Trump to identify his "biggest foe globally right now," Trump responded: "Well, I think we have a lot of foes. I think the European Union is a foe." *Face the Nation*, July 19, 2019, cbsnews.com/news/donald-trump -interview-cbs-news-european-union-is-a-foe-ahead-of-putin -meeting-in-helsinki-jeff-glor/.

2 Quoted from *The Economist*'s English translation of Macron's interview, November 7, 2019. The original French: "L'instabilité du partenaire américain et la montée des tensions font que l'idée d'une Europe de la défense s'installe progressivement. C'est un véritable aggiornamento d'une Europe puissante et stratégique. J'ajoute que nous devrons à un moment faire le bilan de l'OTAN. Ce qu'on est en train de vivre, c'est pour moi la mort cérébrale de l'OTAN. Il faut être lucide." See economist.com/europe/2019/11/07/emmanuel-macron -in-his-own-words-french. For the article based on the interview, see "Assessing Emmanuel Macron's apocalyptic vision," *The Economist*, November 7, 2019, economist.com/leaders/2019/11/07/assessing -emmanuel-macrons-apocalyptic-vision.

3 Philip H. Gordon and Jeremy Shapiro, "How Trump killed the Atlantic alliance," *Foreign Affairs*, February 26, 2019, foreignaffairs.com /articles/united-states/2019-02-26/how-trump-killed-atlantic -alliance.

4   See, for example, Rumi Aoyama, "Japan walks on a tightrope with its China policy," *East Asia Forum*, May 20, 2021, eastasiaforum.org /2021/05/20/japan-walks-on-a-tightrope-with-its-china-policy/; Heung-Kyu Kim, "South Korea's strategic dilemma amid US-China competition," *Stimson Policy Memo*, February 28, 2022, stimson.org/2022/south-koreas-strategic-dilemma-amid-us-china -competition/; Patrick Köllner, "Australia and New Zealand recalibrate their China policies: convergence and divergence," *Pacific Review* 34, no. 3 (2021): 405–36, doi.org/10.1080/09512748 .2019.1683598.

5   Hugh White, "Power shift: Australia's future between Washington and Beijing," *Quarterly Essay* 39 (2010); a shorter version appears in "'Power shift': Rethinking Australia's place in the Asian century," *Australian Journal of International Affairs* 65, no. 2 (2011): 81–93, doi.org/10.1080/10357718.2011.535603, internationalaffairs.org .au/wp-content/uploads/2016/07/Power-shift-rethinking-Australia -s-place-in-the-Asian-century.pdf. See also Hugh White, *The China Choice: Why America Should Share Power* (Collingwood, Au.: Black Inc., 2012; Oxford: Oxford University Press, 2013).

6   United States, *Indo-Pacific Strategy of the United States* (February 2022), whitehouse.gov/wp-content/uploads/2022/02/U.S.-Indo -Pacific-Strategy.pdf.

7   United States, White House, "Fact sheet: Indo-Pacific Strategy of the United States," February 11, 2022, whitehouse.gov/briefing-room /speeches-remarks/2022/02/11/fact-sheet-indo-pacific-strategy-of -the-united-states/.

8   "Evan Feigenbaum: The U.S. and the Indo-Pacific region," transcript of opening remarks to East Asia Strategy Forum 2022, Ottawa, November 1–2, 2022, *Institute for Peace and Diplomacy*, November 18, 2022, peacediplomacy.org/2022/11/18/evan-feigenbaum-the -u-s-and-the-indo-pacific-region/.

9   Japan, Prime Minister's Office, "Keynote address by Prime Minister KISHIDA Fumio at the IISS Shangri-La Dialogue," Singapore, June 10, 2022, japan.kantei.go.jp/101_kishida/statement/202206/_00002 .html.

10 Dina Smeltz, "Japanese public values ties to US, but would prefer to cooperate with China, too," *Chicago Council on Global Affairs*, April 28, 2021, globalaffairs.org/research/public-opinion-survey /japanese-public-values-ties-us-would-prefer-cooperate-china-too.

11 Yukio Hatoyama, "US-China rivalry and Japan's strategic role," *Washington Quarterly* 44, no. 2 (2021): 7–19, doi.org/10.1080 /0163660X.2021.1932093.

12 Yoon Suk-yeol, "South Korea needs to step up," *Foreign Affairs*, February 8, 2022, foreignaffairs.com/articles/south-korea/2022-02 -08/south-korea-needs-step.

13 Jessica J. Lee and Sarang Shidore, "The folly of pushing South Korea toward a China containment strategy," *Quincy Brief 25*, May 5, 2022, quincyinst.org/report/the-folly-of-pushing-south-korea-toward-a -china-containment-strategy/.

14 Asia New Zealand Foundation, *New Zealanders' Perceptions of Asia and Asian Peoples*, June 2022, asianz.org.nz/assets/2021-Perceptions -of-Asia.pdf.

15 Robert Ayson, "New Zealand's foreign policy turnaround," *Incline*, May 20, 2022, incline.org.nz/home/new-zealands-foreign-policy -turnaround; also see Robert Ayson, "New Zealand and the great irresponsibles: Coping with Russia, China and the US," *Australian Journal of International Affairs* 74, no. 4 (2020): 455–78, doi.org/10 .1080/10357718.2020.1734773; Robert Ayson, "New Zealand's alliance obligations in a China-Australia war," *Australian Journal of International Affairs* (2023), doi.org/10.1080/10357718.2023.2177253.

16 See the discussion in Rory Medcalf, *Contest for the Indo-Pacific: Why China Won't Map the Future* (Collingwood, Au.: La Trobe University Press, 2020), 292–302.

17 Angus Thompson, "'Reality of our time': Dutton warns Australian to prepare for war," *Sydney Morning Herald*, April 25, 2022, smh.com.au /politics/federal/reality-of-our-time-dutton-warns-australians-to -prepare-for-war-20220425-p5afuy.html.

18 SSN is the hull classification symbol for nuclear-powered submarines used by both the U.S. Navy and NATO. The vast cost and the long thirty-year time horizon have generated considerable skepticism about the program's sustainability. See, for example, Hugh White, "The AUKUS submarines will never happen," *Saturday Paper* 440, March 11–17, 2023, thesaturdaypaper.com .au/world/2023/03/15/the-aukus-submarines-will-never-happen.

19 Hugh White, "Sleepwalk to war: Australia's unthinking alliance with America," *Quarterly Essay* 86 (2022).

20 Peter Varghese, "US primacy is desirable but it is not a vital Australian interest," *Pearls and Irritations: John Menadue's Public Policy Journal*,

December 15, 2022. johnmenadue.com/us-primacy-is-desirable
-but-it-is-not-a-vital-australian-interest/.

21 Caitlin Byrne, Peter Dean, Stephan Frühling, and Andrew O'Neil,
"'An incomplete project': Australians' views of the US alliance,"
Griffith Asia Institute, ANU Strategic and Defence Studies Centre
and the United States Studies Centre at the University of Sydney,
December 2022, ussc.edu.au/analysis/an-incomplete-project
-australians-views-of-the-us-alliance.

22 Peter K. Lee and Andrew Carr, "Australia's great-power threat
perceptions and leadership responses," *Asia Policy* 17, no. 4 (2022):
77–99, quotation at 99.

23 Emma Shortis, "Imperfect union: Transitioning to an alliance
based on hope, not fear," *Australian Foreign Affairs* 18 (July 2023),
australianforeignaffairs.com/essay/2023/07/we-need-to-talk-about
-america.

24 Trade percentages are approximate and refer to all trade in goods
and services; data from the World Bank's World Integrated Trade
Solutions wits.worldbank.org/, supplemented by data from Japan
External Trade Organization, Korea International Trade Association,
Stats NZ, Australian Department of Foreign Affairs and Trade.

25 Geoffrey Blainey, *The Tyranny of Distance: How Distance Shaped
Australia's History* (Melbourne: Sun Books, 1966).

26 White, "Power shift," 87; in "Sleepwalk to war," 44–69, White
argues that the costs of trying to prevent China from successfully
challenging it in the western Pacific so outweigh the putative
benefits high that Americans will eventually see that their interests
would be better served by stepping back instead.

27 David C. Kang, "Still getting Asia wrong: No 'contain China'
coalition exists," *Washington Quarterly* 45, no. 4 (2022): 79–98,
doi.org/10.1080/0163660X.2022.2148918.

28 This is the perspective of the so-called English School of
International Relations; one of its foundational works is Hedley
Bull, *The Anarchical Society: A Study of Order in World Politics*
(New York: Columbia University Press, 1977).

29 H.R. McMaster and Gary D. Cohn, "America First doesn't mean
America alone," *Wall Street Journal*, May 30, 2017, wsj.com/articles
/america-first-doesnt-mean-america-alone-1496187426.

30 Daniel W. Drezner, "The song remains the same: International
relations after COVID-19," *International Organization* 74 Supplement
(December 2020): E18–E35, doi.org/10.1017/S0020818320000351.

31 Emma Ashford, "It's official: The post–Cold War era is over," *New York Times*, February 24, 2022, nytimes.com/2022/02/24/opinion /ukraine-russia-biden.html.

32 Roland Paris, "We've reached a new post–Cold War era. What follows may be even more dangerous," *Globe and Mail*, March 21, 2022, theglobeandmail.com/opinion/article-weve-reached-a-new-post -cold-war-era-what-follows-may-be-even-more/.

33 Fareed Zakaria, *The Post-American World* (New York: W.W. Norton, 2008; updated 2009; updated and expanded as Release 2.0, 2011).

34 See, for example, Niall Ferguson, *Colossus: The Rise and Fall of the American Empire* (New York: Penguin, 2005); Cullen Murphy, *Are We Rome? The Fall of an Empire and the Fate of America* (New York: Houghton Mifflin Harcourt, 2007).

35 Zakaria, *Post-American World*, 258.

36 Christopher Layne, "The *real* post-American world: The Pax America's end and the future of world politics," in Sean Clark and Sabrina Hoque, eds., *Debating a Post-American World: What Lies Ahead?* (New York: Routledge, 2012), 41–46.

37 For a scholarly exploration, see the contributions to Justin Massie and Jonathan Paquin, eds., *America's Allies and the Decline of U.S. Hegemony* (New York: Routledge, 2020).

6. Navigating a New World

1 Lloyd Axworthy, *Navigating a New World: Canada's Global Future* (Toronto: Knopf Canada, 2003), 6.

2 Roland Paris, "The right to dominate: How old ideas about sovereignty pose new challenges for world order," *International Organization* 74, no. 3 (2020): 453–89, doi.org/10.1017/S0020818320000077.

3 On the patchwork United States that will result, see Tom Nichols, "When democracy ends," *The Atlantic*, January 22, 2022, newsletters .theatlantic.com/peacefield/61e8c5049d9e380022bce4c4/when -democracy-ends/.

4 Matt Viser, "In fiery midterm speech, Biden says GOP's turned toward 'semi-fascism,'" *Washington Post*, August 25, 2022, washingtonpost .com/politics/2022/08/25/fiery-midterm-speech-biden-says-gops -turned-toward-semi-fascism/.

5 The "f-word" debate over whether what is happening in the United States is fascist is extensive. For a compelling, if pessimistic, exploration,

see Anthony R. Dimaggio, *Rising Fascism in America: It Can Happen Here* (New York: Routledge, 2022).

6 George Orwell, "What is fascism?" in *The Collected Essays, Journalism and Letters of George Orwell*, ed. Sonia Orwell and Ian Angus, vol. 3: *As I Please, 1943–45* (New York Harcourt, Brace & World, 1968), 114, mirrored at orwell.ru/library/articles/As_I_Please/english/efasc.

7 Tom Nichols, "Fear of fascism," *The Atlantic Daily*, August 30, 2022, theatlantic.com/newsletters/archive/2022/08/fear-of-fascism/671289/.

8 Barbara Perry and Ryan Scrivens (with Dr. Tanner Mirrlees), "Epilogue: The Trump effect on right-wing extremism in Canada," in Barbara Perry and Ryan Scrivens, *Right-Wing Extremism in Canada* (Cham, Switzerland: Palgrave Macmillan, 2019), 143–71.

9 Eurasia Group, *Top Risks 2023*, 21, eurasiagroup.net/files/upload /EurasiaGroup_TopRisks2023.pdf.

10 John W. Holmes, *Life with Uncle: The Canadian-American Relationship* (Toronto: University of Toronto Press, 1981), 4.

11 K.J. Holsti, "Canada and the United States," in Steven Spiegel and Kenneth Waltz, eds., *Conflict in World Politics* (Cambridge, Mass.: Winthrop Publishers, 1971), 373, quoted in Brian Bow, *The Politics of Linkage: Power, Independence, and Ideas in Canada-U.S. Relations* (Vancouver: UBC Press, 2009), 2.

12 Trump statement, February 4, 2022: twitter.com/AdrianMorrow/ status/1489661479561437186; "Trump criticizes Canada over its removal of convoy protestors in Ottawa," *Globe and Mail*, February 26, 2022, theglobeandmail.com/world/us-politics/article-trump -trucker-convoy-cpac/.

13 Kal J. Holsti and Thomas Allen Levy, "Bilateral institutions and transgovernmental relations between Canada and the United States," in Annette Baker Fox, Alfred O. Hero, Jr., and Joseph S. Nye, eds., *Canada and the United States: Transnational and Transgovernmental Relations* (New York: Columbia University Press, 1976), 283–309.

14 On the IJC, see Daniel Macfarlane and Murray Clamen, eds., *The First Century of the International Joint Commission* (Calgary: University of Calgary Press, 2019), dx.doi.org/10.2307/j.ctvvb7kmv.12.

15 Wilfrid Greaves, "Democracy, Donald Trump and the Canada-US security community," *Canadian Journal of Political Science* 53, no. 4 (2020), 15, doi.org/10.1017/S0008423920000542.

16 See Geoffrey Garrett, "G2 in G20: China, the United States and the world after the Global Financial Crisis," *Global Policy* 1, no. 1

(2010): 29-39; Norman A. Bailey, "Tripolar world: China ascendant?" *Asia Times*, February 6, 2019, asiatimes.com/2019/02/tripolar -world-china-ascendant/; Giovanni Grevi, "The interpolar world: a new scenario," *Occasional Paper* 79, European Institute for Security Studies, June 2009, iss.europa.eu/sites/default/files /EUISSFiles/op79.pdf; Oluwaseun Tella, "Polarity in contemporary international politics: A uni-interpolar order?" *Politeia* 34, no. 2 (2015): 4–23, unisapressjournals.co.za/index.php/Politeia/article /view/659; Niall Ferguson, "A world without power," *Foreign Policy*, October 27, 2009, foreignpolicy.com/2009/10/27/a-world -without-power/; Richard N. Haass, "The age of non-polarity: What will follow U.S. dominance," *Foreign Affairs* 87, no. 3 (2008): 44–56, foreignaffairs.com/articles/united-states/2008-05-03/age-nonpolarity; Ian Bremmer and Nouriel Roubini, "A G-zero world: The new economic club will produce conflict, not cooperation," *Foreign Affairs* (2011), foreignaffairs.com/articles/2011-01-31/g-zero-world.

17   Benjamin Zala, "Polarity analysis and collective perceptions of power: The need for a new approach," *Journal of Global Security Studies* 2, no. 1 (2017): 2–17, doi.org/10.1093/jogss/ogw025.

18   Daron Acemoğlu, "The case for a quadripolar world," *Project Syndicate*, December 3, 2020, project-syndicate.org/commentary/quadripolar -world-better-than-new-us-china-cold-war-by-daron-acemoglu -2020-12.

19   Stephen M. Saideman, "Hegemonic abdication theory," *Saideman's Semi-spew*, December 10, 2017, saideman.blogspot.com/2017/12 /hegemonic-abdication-theory.html.

20   Hayden King, "The erasure of indigenous thought in foreign policy," *Open Canada*, July 31, 2017, opencanada.org/erasure-indigenous -thought-foreign-policy/.

21   The solitude is geostrategic because while Canada has numerous economic and other links with Mexico, the country is not part of the geostrategic West; on the contrary, Mexican governments have always sought to pursue geostrategic independence.

22   John English, "Canada in the post-American world," in Sean Clark and Sabrina Hoque, eds., *Debating a Post-American World: What Lies Ahead?* (New York: Routledge, 2012), 147–51.

23   Roland Paris, "Alone in the world? Making sense of Canada's disputes with Saudi Arabia and China," *International Journal* 74, no. 1 (2019): 151–61, journals.sagepub.com/doi/10.1177 /0020702019834652.

24 Government of Canada, *Canada's Indo-Pacific Strategy* (2022), international.gc.ca/transparency-transparence/assets/pdfs/indo -pacific-indo-pacifique/indo-pacific-indo-pacifique-en.pdf.

25 For example, Maxandre Fortier, Marco Munier, and Justin Massie, "Towards a Canadian strategy in the Indo-Pacific: What to learn from the American and European examples?" *Policy Report* 15 (February 2022), ras-nsa.ca/wp-content/uploads/2022/02/Policy-Report -15-Towards-a-Canadian-Strategy-in-the-Indo-Pacific.pdf; Stephen Nagy, "Canada has pressing interests in the Indo-Pacific. It's time we started acting like it," *The Hub*, June 30, 2022, thehub.ca/2022 -06-30/stephen-nagy-canada-has-pressing-interests-in-the-indo -pacific-region-its-time-we-started-acting-like-it/. Fen Osler Hampson, Goldy Hyder, and Tina J. Park, eds., *The Indo-Pacific: New Strategies for Canadian Engagement with a Critical Reason* (Toronto: Sutherland House, 2022).

26 Kim Richard Nossal, "The North Atlantic anchor: Canada and the Pacific century," *International Journal* 73:3 (2018): 364–78, doi.org /10.1177/0020702018792909.

27 Kari Roberts, "Geopolitics and diplomacy in Canadian Arctic relations," in David Carment and Richard Nimijean, eds., *Canada Among Nations 2020: Political Turmoil in a Tumultuous World* (Cham, Switzerland: Palgrave Macmillan, 2021), 125–46.

28 Thomas Juneau, "Canada will pay the price for neglecting our foreign policy," *Globe and Mail*, June 7, 2020, theglobeandmail .com/opinion/article-canada-will-pay-the-price-for-neglecting-our -foreign-policy/.

29 This was how the late historian Greg Donaghy characterized the attitude of the two allies in the 1960s: see *Tolerant Allies: Canada and the United States, 1963–1968* (Montreal and Kingston: McGill-Queen's University Press, 2002).

30 Graham T. Allison, *Destined For War: Can America and China Escape Thucydides's Trap?* (New York: Houghton Mifflin Harcourt, 2017).

31 Thucydides, *The Peloponnesian War*, trans. Rex Warner (London: Penguin Books, 1954), I, 23.

32 "Highlights of Xi-Obama meeting in Washington DC during Xi's US trip," *China Daily*, September 26, 2015, chinadaily.com.cn/world /2015xivisitus/2015-09/26/content_21989654.htm.

33 Roland Paris, "Navigating the new world disorder: Canada's post-pandemic foreign policy," *Public Policy Forum*, July 16, 2020, ppforum.ca/publications/navigating-the-new-world-disorder/.

34 Greg Donaghy and Thomas Axworthy, "One is the loneliest number: On the world stage, Canada has been left to stand alone," *Globe and Mail*, January 16, 2020, theglobeandmail.com/opinion /article-one-is-the-loneliest-number-on-the-world-stage-canada-has -been-left/.

35 Kerry Buck, "Canada's place in the world is changing. How can it find its footing?" *Maclean's*, January 24, 2022, macleans.ca/politics/canadas -place-in-the-world-is-changing-how-can-it-find-its-footing/.

36 Richard Albert and Allan Rock, "Donald Trump may run, and win, in 2024. Canada must prepare now to protect global democracy," *Globe and Mail*, November 26, 2021, theglobeandmail.com/opinion /article-donald-trump-may-run-and-win-in-2024-canada-must -prepare-now-to/.

37 Scott Gilmore, "The U.S. is sinking. Maybe it's time for Canada to jump ship," *Maclean's*, October 30, 2019, macleans.ca/opinion/the -u-s-is-sinking-maybe-its-time-for-canada-to-jump-ship/.

38 Irvin Studin, "Five moves Canada should make to counter Donald Trump," *Toronto Star*, June 14, 2018, thestar.com/opinion /contributors/2018/06/14/five-moves-canada-should-make-to -counter-donald-trump.html.

39 Robert W. Murray and Tom Keating, "Canada must double down on its multilateral commitments as a new world order emerges," *The Hub*, November 24, 2022, thehub.ca/2022-11-24/opinion-canadian -multilateralism-in-the-new-world-order/.

40 "More cowbell," *Saturday Night Live*, April 8, 2000, nbc.com/saturday -night-live/video/more-cowbell/3506001.

41 For the story of the Third Option, see J.L. Granatstein and Robert Bothwell, *Pirouette: Pierre Trudeau and Canadian Foreign Policy* (Toronto: University of Toronto Press, 1990), 158–77.

42 Canada, Parliament, House of Commons, Standing Committee on Foreign Affairs and International Trade, *Canada and the North American Challenge: Managing Relations in Light of the New Security Environment*, Preliminary Report of the Standing Committee on Foreign Affairs and International Trade, December 2001, 7, ourcommons.ca/Content/Committee/371/FAIT/Reports /RP1032047/faitrp15/faitrp15-e.pdf.

43 Kim Richard Nossal, "Promises made, promises kept? A mid-term Trudeau foreign policy report card," in *Canada Among Nations 2017: Justin Trudeau and Canadian Foreign Policy*, eds. Norman Hillmer and Philippe Lagassé (Cham, Switzerland: Palgrave Macmillan,

2018), 31–53, nossalk.files.wordpress.com/2019/02/nossal_2018
_trudeau-midterm.pdf.

44 Ian Bickis, "Trudeau navigates perils of energy, climate, Trump as
Liberals wrap retreat," *City News*, January 24, 2017, toronto.citynews.ca
/2017/01/24/canada-can-forge-ties-with-trump-while-sticking-up
-for-values-hajdu-says/.

45 Daniel Dale, "Daughter diplomacy: Trudeau's unorthodox play
for Donald Trump's approval," *Toronto Star*, March 16, 2017,
thestar.com/news/world/2017/03/16/daughter-diplomacy-trudeaus
-unorthodox-play-for-donald-trumps-approval.html.

46 David G. Haglund, "*Plus ça change?* France and America during the
Trump interlude," in *Foreign Perceptions of the United States under
Donald Trump*, ed. Gregory S. Mahler (Lanham, Md.: Lexington
Books, 2021), 75–88; William Pesek, "Shinzo Abe decided to go all
out on Donald Trump. He's probably regretting it now," *Washington
Post*, August 29, 2020, washingtonpost.com/opinions/2020/08/29
/shinzo-abe-decided-go-all-out-donald-trump-hes-probably-regretting
-it-now/.

47 Aaron Wherry, *Promise and Peril: Justin Trudeau in Power* (Toronto:
HarperCollins, 2019), 154.

48 Stuart MacKay, "It's time to Trump-proof Canada's foreign policy,"
Hill Times, April 26, 2021, 19, hilltimes.com/story/2021/04/26
/its-time-to-trump-proof-canadas-foreign-policy/268887/.

49 Thomas Homer-Dixon, "The American polity is cracked, and might
collapse. Canada must prepare," *Globe and Mail*, December 31,
2021, theglobeandmail.com/opinion/article-the-american-polity-is
-cracked-and-might-collapse-canada-must-prepare/. See also the
CDA Institute Expert Series interview: "Thomas Homer-Dixon:
Trump's big lie and implications for global democracy," April 13,
2022, youtube.com/watch?v=SU8_84X_CsU.

50 Kim Richard Nossal, "Coming about: Assessing Canada's
geostrategic turn at the end of the post–Cold War era," Canadian
foreign policy blog post, nossalk.files.wordpress.com/2023/04/nossal
_2023_coming-about.pdf.

51 Canada, Department of Foreign Affairs and International Trade,
A Dialogue on Foreign Policy (2002), publications.gc.ca/Collection
/E2-481-2002E.pdf.

52 Roland Paris, "With tectonic international shifts, our foreign affairs
strategy shouldn't be an afterthought," *Globe and Mail*, October
6, 2019, theglobeandmail.com/opinion/article-with-tectonic

-international-shifts-our-foreign-affairs-strategy/; Jean-Christophe Boucher, "Canada's failed Security Council bid marks the death of our traditional foreign policy," *National Post*, June 17, 2020, nationalpost.com/opinion/jean-christophe-boucher-canadas-failed -security-council-bid-marks-the-death-of-our-traditional-foreign -policy.

Conclusion

1   John W. Holmes, *Life with Uncle: The Canadian-American Relationship* (Toronto: University of Toronto Press, 1981), 136.
2   Quoted in David Leyton-Brown, Don Munton, and Kim Richard Nossal, "Political developments in the United States: Sleeping with a different elephant?" Fifth Lester B. Pearson Conference on the Canada–United States Relationship, Niagara-on-the-Lake, 14–17 October 1981, nossalk.files.wordpress.com/2022/12/leyton-brown -and-nossal_1981_sleeping-with-a-different-elephant.pdf.
3   McKay Coppins, "Republicans' 2024 magical thinking," *The Atlantic*, January 30, 2023, theatlantic.com/politics/archive/2023/01 /2024-republican-primary-donald-trump-deus-ex-machina/672888/.
4   Holmes, *Life with Uncle*, 107–8.
5   Robert Draper, *Weapons of Mass Delusion: When the Republican Party Lost Its Mind* (New York: Penguin Press, 2022), xvi.

INDEX

Georgia (country), 40, 105
  Russian war against, 37, 39
Georgia (U.S. state), 64, 68, 71, 80
geostrategic West. *See under* West, the
gerrymandering, 67, 70, 72, 87, 139
Gilead, Republic of, 191n22
"Gileadization," 82
Gilmore, Scott, 156
Gingrich, Newt, 71, 87
Ginsberg, Ruth Bader, 80
global financial crisis, 132, 133
global leadership. *See* American
  global leadership
GoFundMe, 140
GOP. *See* Republican Party
Gorbachev, Mikhail, 33
Gordon, Philip H., 117
Gosar, Paul, 99, 100
Graham, Bill, 163
Graham, Lindsey, 72, 87
Grand Old Party (GOP). *See*
  Republican Party
"great replacement" conspiracy,
  83–84
Greaves, Wilfrid, 144
Greene, Marjorie Taylor, 69, 75,
  99, 101
  advocacy of violence, 80–81
  Christian nationalism, 82, 83
  "gazpacho police," 76, 190n12
  and QAnon, 68, 76
  and Ukraine, 100–101, 102
Greenland, proposed purchase of, 52
Greitens, Eric, 81
Grisham, Stephanie, 51
Gui Congyu, 47
Gui, Michael Minhai, 185n25
"G-zero" world, 145

Haass, Richard, 36

Habermann, Maggie, 54
The Handmaid's Tale, 82, 191n22
Hannity, Sean, 102, 140
Harper, Becky, 70
Harper, Stephen, 28, 30, 152, 163
Harris, Kamala, 1, 84
Hart, Michael, 28
Hatoyama Yukio, 122
Hawley, Josh, 107
"hegemonic abandonment theory,"
  147
hegemonic stability theory, 20
Hice, Jody, 67
Hidalgo, Anne, 2
"hide and bide" strategy, 35, 183n3
Higginbotham, John, 159
Hines, Bo, 64
Holmes, John W., 141, 167
  on dealing with the U.S., 170
Holsti, K.J., 142
Homeland Security, U.S.
  Department of, 144
Homer-Dixon, Thomas, 162
Hong Kong, 43, 46, 47, 109, 151,
  185n25
  Trump on, 58
Hopewell, Kristen, 58
House GOP Conference, 72
  See also Republican Party
Hu Jintao, 41
Huawei Technologies Co. Ltd., 4,
  46, 48, 112, 124
  Australia and, 123–24
  U.S. "war against Huawei," 108
  See also Meng Wanzhou
"human community with a shared
  future," 49, 185n27
Humphrey, John, 26
Hurd, William, 72
hyperpower, 34, 141

INDEX

Stone, Roger, 81, 188n1
"Stop the Steal," 64, 70, 77, 188n1
strategic autonomy, 116, 119, 126,
    130
"Strong, Secure, Engaged," 22, 152
Studin, Irvin, 156
Suez crisis, 23
Summit of Democracies, 156
Sununu, Chris, 64
Supreme Court of the United
    States, 70, 79, 80, 82, 138, 139
systemic war, threat of, 153

Taiwan, 43, 47, 109, 110, 151
    and the geostrategic West,
        18–19, 179n7
    great power war over, 122
Taiwan Relations Act, 19
tariffs
    against Australia, 46
    against Canada, 2, 3, 159–60
    against China, 109, 111, 112
    against U.S. trading partners,
        54, 58, 126
    See also Section 232, Trade
        Expansion Act
Taylor, Miles, 54
Tea Party, 89, 190n12
Texas Heartbeat Act, 81
Third Option, 157
Thomas, Jody, 184n22
"Thucydides trap," 154
Tiananmen Square massacre, 35, 58
Tibet, 43
Trade Expansion Act, 58
Trade Representative, U.S., 144
transgovernmental relations, 143
Transnistria, 39
Trans-Pacific Partnership, 11, 25,
    54, 57

See also Comprehensive and
    Progressive Agreement for
    Trans-Pacific Partnership
Treasury, U.S. Department of, 111
trifectas, 72, 189n9
tripolarity, 145
trucker protest. See "Freedom
    Convoy"
Trudeau, Justin, 2, 7, 8, 149,
    162–63
    and Biden, 4–5
    and Trump, 3, 158–160
Trudeau, Pierre Elliott, 27, 157
    1970 foreign policy review, 164
Trujillo, Audrey, 68
Trump, Donald J. Trump, 1, 8, 9,
    80, 81, 83, 90, 91, 93, 94, 96,
    112, 115, 119, 120, 130, 143,
    152, 155, 169, 170
    2020 election, 60, 64, 65
    2022 mid-terms, 66–68
    alliances, 55–56
    American global leadership, 55,
        60–61, 108, 136
    authoritarianism of, 78–79
    Canadians as "left-wing
        fascists," 143
    China, 108, 109, 111
    climate change, 56–57
    COVID-19, 84
    "deep state," 12
    deplatformed, 102
    domination of Republican
        Party by, 72–76, 86–87
    European Union, 57, 116
    exceptionalism, 59
    as would-be fascist, 138–39
    "Freedom Convoy," 140
    Freeland, 4, 160
    Greenland, purchase of, 52

ABOUT THE AUTHOR

 Kim Richard Nossal was born in London and went to school in Melbourne, Beijing, Toronto, and Hong Kong. His peripatetic schooling was necessitated by his father's profession as an Australian journalist who opened the *Globe and Mail*'s bureau in Beijing in 1959 and then returned to Asia in the mid-1960s to cover the Vietnam War and the cultural revolution in China. After high school Nossal studied at the University of Toronto in the early 1970s; his PhD was supervised by three leading scholars in Canadian foreign policy, John W. Holmes, James Eayrs, and Robert O. Matthews. He joined the political science department at McMaster University in 1976 and taught there for the next twenty-five years before moving to the other end of Lake Ontario in 2001 to become head of the Department of Political Studies at Queen's University. He retired just weeks before the pandemic hit (thus mercifully sparing Queen's students what would surely have been an awkward transition to virtual professoring).

In those forty-three years, Nossal taught courses in International Relations and the intro course in political science, but his main area of study was Canadian foreign policy. He is the author of a number of books, journal articles, and book chapters on that subject, including a standard text in the field, *The Politics of Canadian Foreign Policy*, co-authored with Stéphane Roussel and Stéphane Paquin. This book has been through five editions in English and two editions in French — the most recent French edition published in 2023. In 2018 it was translated into Chinese.

Nossal served as the president of the Canadian Political Science Association in 2005–2006. He was awarded an honorary doctorate by the Royal Military College of Canada in 2017 and was elected as a Fellow of the Royal Society of Canada in 2019. In retirement, he watches the transformation of world politics from Howe Island in the St. Lawrence River.